KT-475-781

Never Rub Bottoms with a Porcupine!

Never Rub Bottoms with a Porcupine!

and other gems from the

NEW STATESMAN
Weekend Competitions 1968-1978

selected and introduced by
ARTHUR MARSHALL

Illustrated by Michael ffolkes

London
GEORGE ALLEN & UNWIN
Boston   Sydney

First published in 1979

This book is copyright under the Berne Convention. All rights
are reserved. Apart from any fair dealing for the purpose of
private study, research, criticism or review, as permitted under
the Copyright Act, 1956, no part of this publication may be
reproduced, stored in a retrieval system or transmitted, in any
form or by any means, electronic, electrical, chemical, mechanical, optical, photocopying, recording or otherwise, without the
prior permission of the copyright owner. Enquiries should be
addressed to the publishers.

This edition © Statesman & Nation Publishing Co. Ltd. 1979

Illustrations © Michael ffolkes 1979

British Library Cataloguing in Publication Data

Never rub bottoms with a porcupine!
  1. English wit and humor   2. English prose
literature – 20th century
  I. Marshall, Arthur   II. 'New statesman'
828'.9'140808   PN6175   79–40028

ISBN 0 04 827019 9

Photoset in Monophoto Baskerville by
Northampton Phototypesetters Ltd
and printed in Great Britain by
William Clowes & Sons Ltd, Beccles and London

FOREWORD

This is the fourth anthology of prize-winning entries in the *New Statesman* Weekend Competitions ('Weekend' only because they originated in the old *Week-End Review*), those challenges to readers to take up their pens or unzip their Olivettis and display their literary skills in a variety of ways but – and this requires an extra, special skill – in a strictly limited number of words. There have, I regret to say, been occasions when the word allowance has, unspotted by the adjudicator, been exceeded by an overexcited competitor and furious rivals have quite rightly written in to complain. Have the word exceeders, covered in shame and confusion, then nobly surrendered their prize-money? Your guess is every bit as good as mine.

The first anthology appeared in 1946, when the ace competition setter and distinguished man of letters, G. W. Stonier, was its editor. The second and third were published in 1955 and 1968 respectively and were compiled by the editor of this 1979 volume. I feel honoured indeed to have had three such anthologies entrusted to me and, as on the previous occasions, I am very happy to express my grateful thanks to the brilliant competitors who have provided me, and indeed all of us, with so many hours of pleasure and of laughter. For the purpose of this 1968–78 volume, I have, as before, reread every entry. It has been an entirely agreeable task.

The choice of item can but be personal. In cases where space has forced me to decide between stunning ingenuity and humour, it is to the latter that I have gone. This has meant including several entries from the same pen or Olivetti but the repetition of winning names has always been a striking feature of the competitions. Among the competitors there have been very few flashes in the pan. Solid reputations have been gradually established over the years, the great names building themselves steadily up week by week – Allan M. Laing, Stanley J. Sharpless, L. E. Jones, R. J. P. Hewison, Edward Blishen and on to such relatively modern phenomena as Russell Lucas and Martin Fagg. There are many more (I could write down at least eighty from memory) and their names have appeared so often because – and remember that they have been judged over many years and by a wide range of people with assorted literary tastes – they are quite simply the best. I give, as usual, a list of the leading prize-winners for each year.

Arthur Marshall

HONOURS BOARDS

The names, in order of merit, of the principal prize-winners in the years 1968–1978.

1968

J. M. Crooks
Martin Fagg
George van Schaick
E. O. Parrott
Roger Woddis
Peter Rowlett
Vera Telfer
Stanley Price
Doris Pulsford
G. J. Blundell
T. Griffiths
Colin Shaw

1969

Martin Fagg
G. J. Blundell
E. O. Parrott
Russell Lucas
J. M. Crooks
Alison Prince
Roger Woddis
Adam Khan
C. Vita-Finzi
Peter Rowlett
T. Griffiths
Michael Russell

1970

Martin Fagg
Roger Woddis
E. O. Parrott
J. M. Crooks
T. Griffiths
Alison Prince
George van Schaick
Russell Lucas
Peter Peterson
Adam Khan
Ian Kelso
C. Vita-Finzi

1971

Martin Fagg
Alison Prince
Stanley J. Sharpless
George van Schaick
Maud Gracechurch
J. D. Crispin
Rufus Stone
G. J. Blundell
Ian Kelso
W. F. N. Watson
J. M. Crooks
Russell Lucas

1972

Martin Fagg
Stanley J. Sharpless
David Phillips
George van Schaick
Maud Gracechurch
T. Griffiths
W. F. N. Watson
Naomi Marks
Alison Prince
E. O. Parrott
John Fuller
Gerry Hamill

1973

Martin Fagg
David Phillips
Naomi Marks
Gerry Hamill
George van Schaick
C. Vita-Finzi
Jack Black
A. M. Sayers
Stanley J. Sharpless
Brian Allgar
Jedediah Barrow
Gerard Benson

1974

Martin Fagg
Naomi Marks
Margaret Rogers
Gerry Hamill
Russell Lucas
G. J. Blundell
M. K. Cheeseman
Brendan Gorse
Jedediah Barrow
Harrison Everard
Adam Khan
Stanley J. Sharpless

1975

Martin Fagg
Harrison Everard
P. W. R. Foot
Basil Ransome
Peter Peterson
C. Vita-Finzi
Stanley J. Sharpless
Naomi Marks
Maud Gracechurch
Colin Kimberley
Gerry Hamill
T. Griffiths

1976

Gerry Hamill
Stanley J. Sharpless
C. Vita-Finzi
Tim Hopkins
Tom Donnelly
Peter Alexander
Jethro B. Tuckett
Russell Lucas
Basil Ransome
Martin Fagg
Tom Brewer
M. K. Cheeseman

1977

Stanley J. Sharpless
Tim Hopkins
Gerry Hamill
Basil Ransome
Moray McGowan
Tom Donnelly
W. S. Brownlie
Peter Peterson
Martin Fagg
T. Griffiths
V. F. Corleone
C. Vita-Finzi

1978

Roy Kelly
Stanley J. Sharpless
Bill Greenwell
T. Hopkins
Robert Baird
Joyce Johnson
Martin Fagg
Gerry Hamill
Jim Anthony
E. O. Parrott
Basil Ransome
Wayne Sidesaddle

1968

BOW, BOW, YE LOWER MIDDLE CLASSES

Social grades made clear

When bicycles stand by the gate,
And Jack the Rocker whets his knife,
And Mum wears curlers in the hall,
And Dad's been put away for life;
When housing's on 'Slum Clearance' lists,
Then cry the Sociologists
                    Non U!
To you, Non U! To us, Grade E,
How unlike us these people be.

When mini cars stand by the gate,
And Bill the budgie pecks his corn,
And Mum puts doyleys on the plate,
And plastic gnomes are on the lawn;
When housing's on the 'Des. Res.' lists,
Then cry the Sociologists
                    Non U!
To you, Non U! To us, Grade C,
How unlike them we hope to be.

When all around the Jags do roar,
And whisky drowns the coq au vin,
And Marion's seat is saddle-sore,
And birds are bronzed from trips to Cannes;
When housing's on 'Historic' lists,
Then cry the Sociologists
                    How U!
To you, How U! To us, Grade A,
How much we'd like to live as they.

J. M. CROOKS

WOGS BEGIN AT CALAIS

Vignettes, likely to give offence, of other peoples

Once one sets aside the distinctive odour of the Syrians, a sort of pleasant rancidity not unlike that of good peanut oil, and once one remembers that we whites reek of milk and starch in the Syrian's nostrils, there is really very little difference to be found between these squat, bluff desert folk and the people of the West. We might well be edified, in fact, by the Syrian's appealingly brusque approach to such elemental actions as defecation. Hunkered easily at the roadside, his honest, patched, and faintly pungent robes hitched up under his armpits, the Syrian reminds us of all the ancient essences our false civilisation has put behind. And when, in the great souk, or bazaar, he smiles his open, unapologetically brown-toothed smile at us from the rear of the unpretentious dirt stall that serves as his home and office, we know we have had the windfall of a profoundly human experience.

RICHARD REID

Your run-of-the-mill Fijian is a cheery sort of cove – honest, obedient and eminently teachable. As a young infantry officer, I had a spell in Suva with a native battalion and managed to muster quite a useful XV from the chaps in my company. Amazing how their performance at the game mirrored their inherent qualities and defects. As plucky as you like as individual runners with the ball (and, of course, they played barefoot!) they had little sense of team play and were abysmal tacklers . . . Then again, though splendid loose ruckers and maulers, their set scrummaging lacked cohesion. No lack of guts, mind – just a lack of that determination and sense of purpose that I, fortunately, was able to impart. After all, a set scrum is one of your few real yardsticks of character left. Call me old-fashioned if you like, but it's my belief that it's only when you've been regularly scrumming down with a chap that you really get to know what he's like, fundamentally.

MARTIN FAGG

FOR THIS RELIEF
MUCH THANKS

**Competitors commented, in sonnet form, on a letter
in the *Sun* which ended with the sentence:
'All our lovely loos are labelled "Ladies".'**

Lav in a Cold Climate

We've had to sell the hall and buy a semi,
Without a single cupboard for the Hons,
And now we find our monde distinctly demi,
Our neighbours just looked blank when offered
                                          scones.
Along their porch six gnomes are standing
                                          gardant,
They call their house a bijou maisonette.
When told I was in pig they murmured
                                    'Pardon?'
And handed me another serviette.
They asked to wash their hands and cried
                                    'How pretty!'
When shown our bathroom suite in lilac mauve,
But the notice on the door we thought so witty
Is *not* considered nice in Laurel Grove –
To show we once lived far above this Hades,
All our lovely loos are labelled 'Ladies'.

J. M. CROOKS

Shall I compare thee to a crap-house door?
You find my new conceit a little strained?
But others found relief through you before,
A thought which leaves me now a trifle pained . . .
I loved you once, but found your entrance bolted
Yet nowadays the casual passing gentry
All passing casual and not revolted
May drop their coin and soon obtain cheap
                                          entry.
Midden, not maiden, who cast my heart adrift,
Another poet suffered once in his turn;
You are my Celia, I your suffering Swift –
I cannot seem to flush you from my cistern.
How apt that on the door that leads to Hades
All our lovely loos are labelled 'Ladies'.

PETER ROWLETT

All our lovely loos are labelled ladies
On Lesbos where the distaff side prevails,
Far from the nightmare world of mainland
                                          Hades
Where monsters stalk disguised as human males.
We do not brook the merging of the sexes
Nor break the law of sexual apartheid:
The crime of incest was not Oedipus Rex's
But joining what our ancient gods divide.
For men and women are two different breeds,
Designed by Fate to live and love apart,
Their bodies separate, and with separate needs,
Each foreign to the other's mind and heart.
Thus is it writ in our advertisements:
'The sunny isle without a single gents.'

ROGER WODDIS

HARD TO SWALLOW

It has been suggested that the Pill is rapidly transforming the female into the sexual predator while having an inhibitory effect upon the male. Tennyson and Keats concurred.

Keep out of the garden, Maud,
   Till your primal urge has flown;
Keep out of the garden, Maud,
   For I'm here in the house alone
And my masculinity's gone by the board
   And the fuse of love is blown.

All night have the moonlit roof-tops high
   Echoed the prowling feet
As the hunting tabbies' hungry cry
   Has wakened the sleeping street
But the silent tom has known to fly
   To his secret dark retreat.

She is coming, my doom, my fate!
   I know that purposeful tread!
My breath is beginning to bate
   And the migraine flies to my head,
My mouth is whispering, 'Wait, O Wait!'
   As I cower beneath the bed.

DOUGLAS HAWSON

White Pill, would I were slippery as thou art –
   Not cradled in my fair love's amorous palm
And watching for her greedy lips to part
   In that new smile, so curious and calm
That turns her face into an antique mask,
   As musing on my potency with pride
She sets me off upon my baffling task
   And through wet, gloomy labyrinths I glide,
No – yet still slippery, it would be my lot
   To leave her fingers, roll beneath the bed,
Hide in the fluff behind the chamber pot
   And let her take another Pill instead,
In the rich dark to crumble and decay,
And so lie ever – or be swept away.

GWEN FOYLE

LET ME INTRODUCE YOU

An unexpected preface to a well-known book

Queen Victoria writes:

A Mrs Emma Lavinia Gifford Hardy recently wrote to us from Dorset, enclosing the manuscript of a novel that she had come across while absent-mindedly going through her husband's desk. She implored us to forbid by Royal Proclamation the publication of what she termed 'this Beelzebub's brew of blasphemous debauchery.' Mrs Hardy is obviously a very *respectable* woman (if a little given to enthusiasm), but we cannot accede to her request, firstly because we have admired many of Mr Hardy's previous productions ('The Trumpet Major' contains some most *respectful* references to our Dear and Illustrious Grandfather) and secondly because, though 'Tess' includes several incidents that must bring a *blush* to any maiden's – nay, to any matron's! – cheek, its general drift is, in our opinion (and We, as a Woman of *Experience*, should know!) not wholly immodest.

There are, in fact, several highly profitable morals to be adduced from this tale of the agreeably frightful Consequences that follow speedily in the wake of moral Error. In the first place, a Young Person, if benighted, should never seek a couch among Leaves or Bracken – particularly if there is the slightest hint of *insobriety* on the part of her companion. Should she be so injudicious as to do so, however, she should stay awake so that she knows exactly What Is Going On!! If, after a Lapse, she should wish to disembarrass herself of her Betrayer, she should never employ a carving knife – a *gross* misuse of domestic cutlery and *not* the sort of thing that could possibly occur in any well-regulated household. All this ends up with poor Tess being *hanged*, and one can only hope that it taught her a good sharp *lesson*! Nor are the other characters free from fault. Angel Clare goes out to farm in Brazil. He comes home very ill, and serve him right! Why could he not go out to farm in Baffin Land or Zanzibar or one of the other priceless jewels in Our Imperial Crown, like any other decent, patriotic English lad . . .

MARTIN FAGG

1969

I'LL SEIZE YOU AGAIN

**The rural eunuchs of Uttar Pradesh complain that
birth control is cutting the income they derive from
singing at birth celebrations. Noël Coward helped them
to provide an anti-sterilisation song for wedding breakfasts.**

Mad dogs and Indians are using the birth control!
This shameful news I uttar
In my falsetto muttar,
In Bombay I've heard them say that nobody pods
at all.
There's scarce a swollen belly
In Delhi . . .
In Hyderabad they are very sad, for there's no-one
under ten,
In Jamshedpur no births occur, for they've sterilised
the men,
In Nagpur the Gossamur is taking a dreadful toll,
For mad dogs and Indians are using the birth
control!

Mad dogs and Indians are using the birth control!
We eunuchs up in Pradesh
Declare the practice caddesh,
In Madras a piece of ass is pleasure and nothing
more,
In loop-bedevilled Lucknow
They're stuck now . . .
Up in old Assam they don't give a damn, they just
sit round drinking tea,
But you must abide by the bareback ride or I face
redundancy.
Though eunuch, I wish you luck, or I'll soon be
drawing dole
Now mad dogs and Indians are using the birth
con, using the birth con, using the birth control!

PETER ROWLETT

BRIEFLESS ENCOUNTER

The American Sunbathing Association has decided to make a promotional film with 'tastefully done nude scenes' in an effort to improve public attitudes towards nudity. Competitors suggested tasteful scenes or dialogue for use in the film.

(ASA amendments in parentheses)

Scene: A bridge table, with four tastefully unclad naturalists, two male and two female, arranging their hands. (The table must have a glass top: our psychological consultants advise us that concealment of the genital areas of otherwise naked bodies is liable to deprave and corrupt. Hence we would suggest an aerial shot.)

NORTH: Pass. (We feel that the British usage 'no bid' would be better here: the word 'pass' has unfortunate sexual connotations.)

EAST: One no trump. (This is acceptable as long as no undue emphasis is placed on the last four letters of the word 'trump'. Perhaps 'one NT' would be safer.)

SOUTH: Double. (Substitute a suit bid: we are anxious to dispel the impression that our clubs encourage alcoholic orgies and the word 'double' has other connotations for non-bridgeplayers.)

WEST: Two spades. (Could this be 'two diamonds'? It must be obvious that we do not condone racialism in any form: 'spade', we believe, may offend certain ethnic groups.)

ALAN ALEXANDER

PICTURE OF A ROSE

This is a rose. It is naked. A rose, as you probably know, wears no clothes. Nor does
PICTURE OF BUTTERCUP
a buttercup. Or
PICTURE OF SKUNK
a skunk.
A loaf of bread does not wear clothes either.
PICTURE OF COTTAGE LOAF
except when it's wrapped.
A WRAPPED LOAF APPEARS ALONGSIDE
Which tastes better, is more nutritious – is crunchier?
THE COTTAGE LOAF BOUNCES UP AND DOWN
Bunnies are naked. Doggies are naked. Pussies are naked.
THE PETS BOUND IN ON THEIR NAMES
Society does not seem to mind naked children.
A NAKED BABY COOS AND BLOWS BUBBLES
TWO TWO-YEAR-OLDS PADDLE IN A SUNSET TO 1,000 VIOLINS AND 2,000 HARPS.
Why should not we allow that nakedness in humans is beautiful? Rubens did. So did Michelangelo, Botticelli, Raphael, Titian, Leonardo da Vinci . . .
WE GET A SURVEY OF WORLD ART UP TO 18th CENTURY IN TWO MINS FLAT
Is it fair to give to the rose, the buttercup and the skunk what we give to our kith and kin when the artists of the world have featured it so much? Why can we view in the Art Gallery what we will not permit in Times Square?

M. K. CHEESEMAN

NEVER RUB BOTTOMS WITH A PORCUPINE!

According to a *Guardian* correspondent, an Ashanti proverb says: 'Do not rub bottoms with a porcupine.' Further proverbs or aphorisms were invented of an equally self-evident nature.

You make few friends by driving northwards on a southbound carriageway.

LT COL W. F. N. WATSON

Many hands make a tall horse.

MICHAEL RUSSELL

If there's no lead in your pencil you don't need a rubber.

J. A. SMITH

Tomorrow is what today was yesterday.

R. ARMSTRONG

He who has the biggest feet will cover the most ground.

ALISON PRINCE

Gloves make a poor present for the man with no hands.

GEORGE VAN SCHAICK

One does not moisten a stamp with the Niagara Falls.

P. W. R. FOOT

A bald man does not fear grey hair.

T. GRIFFITHS

He digs deepest who deepest digs.

ROGER WODDIS

A new dishwasher can't mend a broken heart, but it will do the washing-up.

ADAM KHAN

Seek not cherry blossom on the plum tree.

BRIAN RICHARDS

Do not wear earmuffs in the land of the rattlesnake.

N. J. ROCK

A knowledge of Sanskrit is of little use to a man trapped in a sewer.

He whose head resembles a Dutch cheese does not rest it on the grocer's counter.

C. H. W. ROLL

A bird in a taxi's worth two in a bus.

G. R. McFARLANE

Even nuns are screwed in their coffins.

RUSSELL LUCAS

JUST NOT SO STORIES

It has been suggested that the story of Peterloo, if not entirely mythical, has been greatly exaggerated for Radical propaganda purposes. Competitors were invited to provide inside stories exposing the myth of the Black and Tans and the Slave Trade.

How well I remember calling at Coole that sun-soaked day in June, 1919, to collect Lady Gregory, Yeats and the widowed Maud MacBride (*née* Gonne) for a picnic. Yeats, his habitual oddity of attire heightened by infatuation, had absent-mindedly donned a black frock-coat plus the khaki trousers belonging to Friggit, his cockney manservant newly demobbed from Flanders – Friggit being obliged to combine a khaki tunic with his master's black trousers.

The Crossley tender, which I had just bought at an Army surplus sale at Cork to tow behind my 1911 De Bouton, proved a superb open tourer and as we wound between the soft blue hills, there was scarcely a sound save that of the curlews crying, Lady G. quietly practising her Erse irregular verbs, and Yeats repeatedly – but, alas, unsuccessfully! – proposing to Maud ('Don't be so *silly*, Willie,' she kept murmuring).

Having lost our way, we stopped in a village where, eyed suspiciously by the peasantry, Yeats and his man were just clambering down to enquire our whereabouts when the catastrophe occurred. A crate of Cassidy's famous 'Fortified Ginger Beer', stowed beneath the driver's seat and volatilised no doubt by the heat and movement, exploded with fearful effect – three bottles going smack through the engraved plate glass of 'O'Houlihan's Select Bar and Snug' while a fourth demolished the priest emerging from the church of 'Our Lady of Fatima'.

We recovered our wits to see the entire population of the village legging it away through the bog to Ballycrumpet, full of dire tales of a posse of particoloured assassins in army trucks unleashed upon them by the 'murdherin' English'. When the rumours reached Dublin, Michael Collins's propaganda boys lost no time at all . . .

TIM O'DOWDA

Interviewed today, Mrs Hagar Ffoulkes of Takoradi said: 'The British Hulk Trading Association are doing a grand job. My husband, family of four and myself have all been placed in holiday homes. No, we don't pay a penny. We live as family. Later, I believe, exchanges are to be arranged so that colonists out here can see our beautiful country. The children are about twenty miles away on another plantation. It is the first holiday from the children that I have had since they were born. Of course I help out in the house. It is the least I can do in return for the hospitality that we have received here. Yes, the iron collar is free, too . . .'

EILEEN M. HAGGITT

Music and myth strike to the same ganglion of feeling, so it is appropriate that music should have spawned that most inveterate of myths, the Slave Trade. When the court band of the jovial 27-stone King Jass of the Lower Niger was, in 1699, seduced into sailing for New Orleans by an exceptionally opulent contract, their arrestingly new kind of music (loyally named after the eupeptic monarch) proved so deliriously popular among the planters that impresarios were soon bringing over many boatloads of African musicians a month. Many, to while away the passage, whipped themselves into such frenzies of inspired improvisation that they expired before landfall, giving rise thereby to all manner of calumnious rumours. The auctions at which, when they arrived, their services were frantically bid for by the jazz-crazy plantation owners have also been most scandalously misrepresented. In their land of adoption, the erstwhile subjects of King Jass proved as fertile genetically as melodically – further evidence of their pampered reception. Only Yankee arrogance, refusing to concede that any good thing could come out of the South, prevented delicious julep-cool jazz from percolating to the ears of the world until the early decades of this century.

IAN KELSO

I KNEW YOU HAD IT IN YOU

An American psychiatrist claims that dizziness, headaches, colitis, flatulence and peptic ulcers are really poems struggling to be born. Competitors were invited to go into labour.

Ode to the South Wind:

me heartburn an' a lousy glumness irks
me guts an' seems to fair bung up me works;
me palpitations comes in fits an' jerks
as if a furkin' gherkin in me lurks:
with dizzy spells an' stabbin' pains like dirks
I feel as good fer nothin' as them berks
as ponce around, all talk an' teeth an' smirks
chattin' up mini-skirted wimmin clerks.
this skyatrist 'e reckons, in the circs,
it's just a question of me mental quirks;
in pod with rhymes, 'e says; an' if I shirk
expressin' it in verse I'll go berserk.
I'll try it on. I feel a proper twit;
but take me ballpen now an' press the tit
an' write O Muse relieve this burstin' heart
begod she did an' cured me, with a fart!

TOM BREWER

HAY FEVER

Time to pass
tempting grass
pollen count
yet I mount
bit of fluff
sneeze and stuff.
Under trees,
grunting wheeze.
Jerk again,
pray for rain.
Home in grief
no relief
seeds abound
head goes round
cat on lap
nasal clap.
End I must
dust to dust!

COLYN DAVIES

24

I have been
reading about
   the reason I
     get seedier and seedier;
       it's all down here in this
         informative encyclopaedia.
         The stomach – it says – is a large muscular receptacle
         which, under particular circumstances, is susceptacle
         to gastric disorders known as peptic or duodenal ulcers
         (these occur when you are fraught and your financial assets are null, sirs).
         The stomach is shaped rather like this digestory ditty,
         which means, I'm afraid, that it doesn't confess to be pretty.
         Of course, in a sheep, this tiresome but necessary bag is,
         for reasons best known to the Scots, called a haggis,
       and, as everyone knows, celebrated on Burns Night is –
     (you can also get another complaint called gastro-enteritis)
   If I have got an ulcer peptic or otherwise,
through worry or overeating, I shall have to
think twice before I eat caviare or even buy it,
or avocado pear or other items of normal diet;
   such delectable comestibles
   are indigestibles.
We are now at
the pylorus;
the chorus
could extend
   down the
       twenty odd
         feet of
           the tube
           called
             intest-
               inal, but
                  that trip
                   (for food)
                     is part-
               icularly
           fi-
        nal.

EILEEN M. HAGGITT

IDEAL HOMES

Unusual architectural conversions

With its red tiled roof rising steeply above a dense thicket of holly and laurel, no one could ever take Viola Cottage for anything but a traditional British public lavatory. In fact it is now the home of a typical English couple. Ronnie Tupp is a wallpaper designer and Jeff Pratt works on a building site to get material for the one-act plays he writes for television.

'The council wanted us to have that place on the Embankment,' said Ronnie, 'but we stuck out for this one. It's where we first met.'

J. REES

A unique experiment in linear living is discoverable in North Wales, where Gordon and Megan ap Thomas have set themselves up in the 989-yard-long tunnel under Cader-y-Clwyd, recently declared surplus to British Rail.

'Gordon is up the mountain,' said attractively pale Mrs ap Thomas, 'picking sheep's wool off the BBC-2 aerial. It's getting more and more homelike here. We grow our own salt and edible toadstools. I'm old-fashioned enough to want a back door, even if it does make the spare bedroom 826 yards long. The wall niches could be useful, but there are 206 of them, and we only use one as a cupboard. We really need 205 statues. Of course, there's no drainage, but we're quite used to the earth closet. It's just outside the back door – a bit far and a little noisy if Gordon gets up in the night: he has to use his motor bike. Actually we could find room for someone to share – say a tall unmarried mother. Or a long one – it's the same thing, isn't it? Not that we're lonely – we could do with some help on rug-knitting.'

MARTIN JORDAN

Norman Quatorze is in interior decorating himself. 'As soon as I took in the atmosphere of this place, I was in no doubt what the dominant colour had to be. Blood. What else could one use for an old abattoir?' What indeed? Some of the walls resolutely refused to be stripped of the deposits of the years. 'Not that I wanted to clean them everywhere,' explained Norman. 'I didn't want to interfere with anything in the dining-room, which was the old bullock-chamber. One couldn't reproduce that marvellous patina in a thousand years.' I asked him about the odour of the untreated walls, but he confessed laughingly that he himself used too much after-shave lotion to be affected. 'So do all my friends,' he added, with a smile. The atmosphere of the original building has been preserved by Norman's clever use of natural cow-hide and sheep-skin, married to simple block-like forms for tables and chairs. 'Blood-stained' curtains are hung from real meat-hooks and his latest innovations are some plastic mobiles, designed to look like the insides of slaughtered animals. 'I had "Guts", as I call these, made for myself originally but I'm putting them out commercially as well,' said Norman. 'Now everyone's after my "Guts".'

E. O. PARROTT

ASKING FOR A RISE

The success of the *Which?* supplement on contraceptives suggested a similar one on aphrodisiacs.

Aphrodisiacs are for men (but are often bought by women for men). Do they really work? If so – how quickly and for how long? The folklore is unreliable so we tried to find out.

We tested 18 aphrodisiacs. 12 were chemical, five mechanical and one electrical.

Of the 12 chemical compounds we tried, 10 were taken by mouth (two powders, seven potions, one lozenge), one was introduced intravenously by syringe, and one was rubbed into the scalp like brilliantine.

All five of the mechanical devices (two clockwork, two elastic, one compressed air) were durable, rustproof and safe but tended, after a time, to generate an affection for the appliance itself which we thought undesirable, so we do not recommend them.

Only one electrical apparatus (The Wiltmaster) was thought safe enough for inclusion and that had no suppressor.

Two further aids (a herbal locket and a pair of impregnated socks) we found impossible to evaluate as so much depended on the suggestibility of the wearer. But they are cheap and you might like to try them for yourself.

GERALD HINCH

At the beginning of the research, it was decided to test not merely purchasable preparations, but all those other formulae sent in by members of the public who had found them efficacious. So copious was the tide of elixirs, tinctures and other nostra that began to flow in to the Research Centre after the first announcement that we had to engage fresh testers, some of whom had shortly afterwards to drop out for various reasons, among the more interesting of these being: total paralysis (four cases); sterility (three); accelerated senile decay (three); apoplexy (two); insanity (two); death (one). A lamentable setback to our researches occurred when, after the Project Director had himself volunteered to test a particularly intriguing recipe sent in by a public-spirited mother of 19 from Upton Maltravers, there was, it appears, a certain amount of unpleasantness on an underground train stopped temporarily, through a technical fault, in a tunnel just outside Belsize Park Station. Naturally, we at the Centre regret that neither the 13 ladies involved nor the judge at the Old Bailey felt able to take a sufficiently detached view of the incident for the Director to be restored to us, but we are nevertheless grateful to the authorities at Pentonville for permitting him to continue to afford us useful assistance with the card-indexing.

MARTIN FAGG

NOTHING AGAINST YOU PERSONALLY

An employer turned down a coloured school-leaver applicant with the words 'Your pigmentation would make you more allergic to frostbite in our frozen foods'. Similarly tactful turndowns were asked for.

Dear Mr Jones,

It is with regret that we have to terminate your employment with us; but your week's trial has proved unsatisfactory. The fault may lie with us: at your interview we felt that if a perfect niche did exist for a boot-fetishist it was in a shoe-shop. We admit that no other employee has ever shown such devotion to our wares – none, for instance, has ever given a pet name to every shoe in the place or arranged a mock-marriage between a right and left brogue – but we began to doubt your vocation during your period in the stockroom. No amount of chits could induce you to release the stock; moreover, you ordered 40 dozen pairs of steel-tipped clogs, more than a Bond Street store could reasonably dispose of. As a salesman your technique lacked finesse – clients come to inspect our shoes, not for you to examine their feet. You were mistaken to attack the gentleman with the scuffed toecaps, and wrong to call him a sadist. And customers find it disturbing to encounter, on entering the shop, a salesman who clutches at their feet and offers large sums to be allowed to purchase the shoes they arrived in.

It is with reluctance that we make the decision to dismiss you. Please do not feel that this occurrence in any way debars you from doing business with us. Enclosed you will find your insurance cards and our Spring catalogue.

PETER ROWLETT

I'm awfully sorry, dear. I did tell them boys only – not that I've anything against you personally, mind. Us girls have to stick together, I always say. No, it's the budgie.

He first started when I was going to those navigation classes when we were going to go on the Broads. Bill said he must have got it from the telly but I never heard them say things like that, not even on BBC-2. I told Bill, I said, I don't like to be suspicious but I do feel he's heard something in *this very room*. Because it's only when a girl comes near him he starts.

So you do see, dear, don't you? It just wouldn't be *nice* for you, living with a bird like that. It's different for me. I've come to understand his little ways.

ALISON PRINCE

Now lass, I know you're set on becoming a first class grout stopper's cockle brusher, but you see, at the end of the apprenticeship comes the Berking Out ceremony and the Grout Master won't pass anyone who hasn't been properly berked. The lads are stripped, shaved, coated with Templers Number Two and whipped three times round the yard with strips of teasel. And then . . . well, this is where you'd be at a cruel disadvantage. Before their papers are signed they have to drink a yard of brown ale and – from ground level mind – pee over the foundry wall.

J. REES

Dear Mr Dainty,
   Much as I appreciated your frankness at our interview yesterday, I fear I am unable to offer you a job here.
   As you know, we manufacture confectionery. Unfortunately several of the phrases that are in daily and inevitable use in a sweet factory – 'just a minty bit stronger', 'a really chewy fruitgum', 'a case of liquorice allsorts' and 'I wouldn't mind a lick at your sherbet dab' – have in recent years acquired connotations that might lead you to suppose that your work-mates, in employing such locutions, were making invidious references to yourself.
   As you are obviously extremely sensitive (a fact you were good enough to volunteer no fewer than seven times in the course of our brief interview) I think you will agree that it is better that you should not join us.

Yours sincerely,
Gordon John
(Personnel Manager)

P.S. I do hope the split you sustained in your very striking pair of electric pink jeans when you were kind enough to sit on the corner of my desk in the course of our conversation did not incommode you unduly on your way home in the Tube.

TIM O'DOWDA

ABSENT FRIEND

**Competitors commented in various ways on the demise
of the Queen's Christmas Day broadcast.**

Oh with what sadness and consternation
Did our grief-stricken nation
Learn that this year
Our beloved Queen was not to have her say
On Christmas Day!
In factories and offices, among people of every
                                          station,
It was the one topic of conversation;
And many could not forbear to shed a tear
Because those well-known accents were not as
              usual to ring out loud and clear
Over the television and the radio
To make us gasp in admiration, 'Oh!'
Ah, unwonted and unlooked-for deprivation!
How shall each
Loyal citizen be able to digest his
Christmas dinner without that accustomed
                                          speech,
Which was, so to speak, the mustard
To the fowl, and the plum pudding's custard?
Oh bring back those noble accents once again,
And save us listeners from a lot of pain!

G. J. BLUNDELL

Quen gorgeit fow wi dainte dennar
Til sicht of it brenges on a scunnar,
Then coms my Yuilles felicite.
Regina non conturbit me.

The clokkes handes the hour is nie;
I stretcche my legges and clos myne e;
The brattis are husht and peis reignes fre;
Regina non conturbit me.

Anon her voce pypes shril and cleir.
Anon doonfals a myrthfow teir.
Tho she say nocht thats worth a fle,
Regina non conturbit me.

Allace, the dames wil skryke this yeir,
And bernis bickar in myne eir.
Nae respit; reuth it so suld be,
Regina non conturbit me.

ANNA JONES

Good Queen Lizzie will not speak
On the feast of Santa,
She will spend her Christmas week
Riding at a canter.

'Secretary, where's my script,
Full of gracious pratings?
Where my smile, anaemic-lipped?
What about our ratings?'

'Ma'am, although we hold you dear,
We are Boxing clever,
Like the snows of yesteryear,
You are gone forever.

We have heard those well-worn words
Annually uttered,
Chosen pearls before the herds,
Words like parsnips – buttered.

Still, we'll find another spot,
Be no longer solo!
You and Phil could earn a lot
Advertising Polo.'

PETER ROWLETT

VICAR'S DOINGS EXPOSED

To combat the declining circulation of parish magazines, competitors were asked to give somewhat racier treatment to various items – the serial story, local church news, etc.

DAISY GRUNT: NEW FACTS

It was just an ordinary Women's Guild meeting until Mrs Daisy Grunt, the attractive widow from the sweetshop, burst in with her clothing in disarray. The story she sobbed out to 20 shocked matrons led to the unfrocking of the Rev. Stephen Codsroe, then vicar of our church.

Mrs Grunt, well known to readers as our deputy organist, has decided to reveal, exclusively in St Anselm's Parish News, hitherto unknown facts about that fateful afternoon five years ago.

Some may argue that Mr Codsroe has paid for his sins. Indeed, the Bishop has already tried to deny Daisy Grunt the right to speak out frankly and fearlessly.

But we think the parishioners of St Anselm's are adult enough to be told the facts and Christian enough to form a fair judgment. Order your copy of next month's Parish News now. And God be with you.

PETER VEALE

Perdita gazed at the curate eagerly as he struggled with the mobile pulpit. Beads of sweat were standing out on his pale nose just under the place where the cruelly gripping pince-nez cut into his flesh. A long, delicious groove showed in his neck where the dog collar made its mark and his body strained under its tight black clothes as he grappled with struts and wing nuts.

'Oh please, can I help?'

'No. Thank you very much, but I wish –'

'What?'

'Nothing. Nothing at all.'

He was divine when he was angry.

At last the pulpit was erected and the curate climbed up, Bible in hand. Perdita stared at his feet, encased in their tight-laced black shoes. Leather shoes.

'In the name of the Father and of the Son and of the Holy Ghost,' began the curate, 'let us consider our sins. My theme for this afternoon is Punishment.'

Perdita closed her eyes blissfully. At last. It had been Brotherly Love for the last three weeks.

ALISON PRINCE

DARBY AND JOAN CLUB

More than 40 senior citizens assembled in the Parish Hall last Thursday afternoon for their monthly freak-out. The proceedings opened quietly with the Vicar's usual reading of selections from the Sunday papers, but livened up when Miss Parslow led the meeting in a number of Rugby Songs. Then Mesdames Harrison and Jones performed an inventive strip-tease which drew loud applause from those still capable of movement. Tea was provided by Mesdames Elfin, Coote, and Brickett, that 'little something extra' in the cakes being added by Miss Harcourt. Miss Wilson then described a chance meeting in her youth with King Edward VII. After a final round of 'Pelt the Parson', from which the Vicar was fortunate to emerge with only superficial injuries, the meeting dispersed.

FERGUS PORTER

HELLO WORLD

Famous first words at birth

HAROLD WILSON: This is Labour's best result so far.

MARIE STOPES: This need never have happened.

F. A. V. MADDEN

MRS MARY WHITEHOUSE: If I'd known that there was any sex involved, I wouldn't have agreed to have come.

E. O. PARROTT

DR SPOONER: Now for a nab at the gripple!

PETER PETERSON

HAROLD WILSON: I knew there was light at the end of the tunnel.

HARRY HODGKINSON

HOUDINI: The rest should be easy.

R. A. K. WRIGHT

ROMULUS: What big teeth you have, Grandma.

MRS A. MACINTYRE

ATTLEE: A not altogether uninteresting experience.

MARTIN FAGG

OEDIPUS: I'll be back.

ROGER WODDIS

DE GAULLE: Get those shepherds out of here.

DICK BIRD

CHARLES I: I don't like sticking my neck out.

L. G. UDALL

JULIUS CAESAR: *Haec sectio Caesariana nominabitur.*

HARTLEY THWAITE

ENOCH POWELL: Oh my God! An immigrant doctor.

JESUS: My father was never in these parts.

GERALD HINCH

A FRIEND WRITES

Extracts from the obituary of any well-known person as he would probably write it himself

BERNARD MONTGOMERY, Field Marshal; never suffered fools; no time for nonsense, self-indulgence, smoking, sex, slackness, drink, sentimentality. Always fit as a flea. Strategy and tactics thoroughly competent; knocked Rommel for six. Wrote a bit. Always put up a good show. Detested long-windedness. Died.

W. F. N. WATSON

During the Second World War he had the honour to be Deputy Prime Minister of the wartime Coalition Government under the inspired leadership of Sir Winston Churchill. He found this very interesting, giving as it did the opportunity to meet many interesting men and women who were in the forefront of the councils of the world. He also travelled extensively at this time, which was also very interesting. After the war, he had the honour to head the post-war Labour Government, which was a very interesting time for him, bringing him further chances to meet interesting people and visit interesting places at home and overseas. The Labour Party under him was able to pass some useful legislation which had some effect on the country as a whole. Later, he had the honour to become an Earl and was active for some years in the House of Lords, which was very interesting as well.

M. K. CHEESEMAN

Ah now, Francis was a comic. And a very comical fellow he was, too. They called him the Titular King of the Clubs, you know. Yes, and a more titular king you never saw. Course, he couldn't be bothered with the money – meant nothing to him. Just as well, considering what the BBC paid him. 'Howerd', they would say – yes, like that. Some of them spent so much time looking down their noses they developed tunnel vision. 'Howerd, an excellent performance – take these coins with our thanks'. Coins! Coins! A pittance. A pit-tance. No ants were ever pittier. No, it wasn't funny. Course, he was carried off in his prime. He departed this vale of tears in the very prime of his young life. Bright-eyed, vibrant, saucy – saucy! Well he came from Worcester, you see; it was bred into him. Only 28, you know. Yes, well the suffering aged him so . . .

JOHN GARRETT

We annce. wth. rgrt. sudd. dth. ydy. Mr J. Dltn., fndr., prop., and mnging. ed. of *Dltn's. Wkly.*, wkly. pub. ddcated. to ads. Mr Dltn., wh. lves. 1 wfe. & 3 child., ws. fr. mny. yrs. dvted. to pub. of ads., an art whch. he mde. partly hs. own. Strtng. as off. by. & tea-mker. at the *Dly. Tel.*, he evtlly. sved. engh. mon. to strt. Dltn's. Snce. thn., he nver lked. bck. He lved. smply. in des. mod. hse. in Hamp. Gdn. Sub. (2 recep., 4 bed., mod. kit., bath., sep. w.c.; cent. hting; lge, gdn. with 6 gnms. (1 fshing)). Hbbes. incl. hols. & cllctng abbrevs. He wll. be mssd. by lge. no. frnds. & rels.

MAUD GRACECHURCH

NOVEL VIEWS

A recently published novel from the Continent refers to Wimpy Bars as though they were fashionable haunts of the jet set. Competitors provided excerpts from other novels betraying equally subtle feelings for the nuances of the contemporary English scene.

A surging excitement filled Natasha as the tall young revolutionary led her through the wintry streets of the capital. She saw the patient, starved faces of the workers obediently lining up for the transports to take them back to their tenements. Soon – sooner than they could dream – they would be freed forever from their Capitalist-Wilsonist oppressors. 'West-Minster' she espied on a street-name – the very heart of the enemy stronghold. The cold air shivered with the stern chimes of Big-Ben, the great clock atop the government offices. Doubt assailed her again: but where were the arms to come from for the uprising? As if hearing her unspoken question her companion made for a great building whose tall windows blazed with light.

Inside, Natasha blinked in amazement. Before her eyes were row upon row of rifles, mortars, field-pieces, mitrailleuses, Maxim Guns and – floating gracefully on a sunken pool – a gun-boat with steam up.

Ecstatically she pressed her companion's arm. 'But how –'

He smiled. 'Every Londoner knows where to find the Army and Navy Stores.'

PHILIP PURSER

On Carmen's first morning in England, John decided to take her to town. At the station, warm and pleasant in the May sunshine, they were soon joined by other commuters. They walked past the bookstall and the antirrhinum beds, as far as the cycle shed, then back again, giving polite 'Good morning's' to John's friends and admiring the trendy wear of the typists. Still the train did not arrive, so John suggested coffee at the buffet.

'You spend *every* day so charming a "paseo"?' asked Carmen.

'Every day,' said John, 'and again at night.'

'Such healthy English ways!'

When the train came, it was two coaches short. The hundred passengers squeezed into 'Seats for Ten'. Carmen snuggled between John's arms and the broad back of a retired colonel.

'My duenna should be here,' she whispered, her eyelids a-flutter.

'Don't worry. If you feel like fainting, lean back on the next fellow. He won't let you down.'

'So loyal, you Englishmen!' murmured Carmen.

N. J. ROCK

Double yellow lines at the sides of village roads serve an odd purpose. Our driver, recognising them as guide-lines, followed them with great care for half a mile. At this point he drove into a muddy field where a notice said that each of the thousand cars must pay ten shillings. We tried to explain that we did not wish to see a field, but the thing in the village. The driver told us to go back along the yellow lines walking. Being Tibetans, we did not mind the walk but we could not understand why we should have to go away from a place just to get back to it. Half an hour later we understood.

The 'site' was a stone in a yard where one of their dukes had lost his head. We could not see any blood on the stone, but every one of the twenty restaurants, full of Americans eating cream teas, was anxious to serve us. It was just a trick to make us hungry.

A. B. GETHING

BEYOND OUR FACULTIES

Competitors suggested new courses for universities with an ideological or other justification for their inclusion.

'I took the course in Telerision,' said the Mock Turtle.

'Don't you mean Television?' inquired Alice in puzzled tones.

'No, I mean Telerision,' said the Mock Turtle impatiently. 'From Tele and Derision.'

'Oh, you mean making mock,' said Alice.

'Of course he does,' exclaimed the Gryphon, waving a paw irritably. 'That's why he's called a Mock Turtle.'

'What was the syllabus?' asked Alice.

'Not syllabus,' said the Mock Turtle crossly. 'Sillybus. We had to learn Expert-Tease, Tele-comics, Politicklers and Mirthematics.'

'I've never heard of those,' said Alice.

'You *are* a simpleton,' said the Gryphon with a sigh. 'I'll have to explain, I suppose. Expert-Tease means putting awkward questions to an expert. Politicklers is the same, only on Panorama.'

'Then there was Divine Comedy,' interrupted the Mock Turtle. 'You know, religious discussions about celibacy and such things.'

'How can a serious programme like that be comical?' asked Alice wonderingly.

'Really you *are* dull!' exclaimed the Gryphon. 'The serious ones are the funniest.'

ROGER WODDIS

A Parisian countess, returning from Proust's funeral, encountered a friend who, on learning where she'd been, remarked: 'Marcel Proust? Who's he?' Suddenly, the countess records, she felt *'une immense fatigue'*. Your Faculty, having pondered many hundred doctoral theses with titles like: 'The Tensile Heart: Patterns of Moral Equilibrium in the Poetry of Emily Dickinson', confesses to sensations of similar weariness. It has decided therefore to scrap the existing ENGLIT course and substitute for it an anonymous happening. Anyone who wishes will be lent a selection of books that some people in the past have found meritorious and will be given a quiet, warm room (adequately stocked with alcohol, tobacco, coffee, etc.) in which to read them. There will be no lectures, seminars or tutorials, nor will there be any terminal examinations, gradings or assessments. The 'course' will have no objective, produce no result and will provide no marketable qualification whatsoever. Your Faculty has meanwhile awarded itself a well-earned sabbatical and will be engaged in literary research in Las Vegas.

MOLLY FITTON

1970

TO HAVE AND TO HOLD

Further well-known personalities provide subject-matter for the 'me and my mate' series currently popular in the press.

Smiling quietly while body-servants massaged him with confident skill, Prasutagus told me that it was Boadicea who married him, rather than the other way round. 'There was no doubt that she had her eye on me from the start', he said, adding, 'It was rather flattering'. Our conversation was interrupted by a servant who brought us mead in a goblet delicately wrought. 'Something my wife looted from the Romans', explained Prasutagus. 'The mead or the goblet?' I enquired. 'Both', came the smiling reply. As we sipped the sweet liquid, I asked whether his wife had any irritating mannerisms. He said that he had initially disliked her habit of keeping two horses fully-saddled in the bedroom at all times, 'in case of attack'. He followed my thoughts quickly. 'By the Romans, of course', he said. Hung about the walls were some of the discarded blades from the Queen's chariot. Proudly, Prasutagus listed the battles in which they had been used and the casualties they had caused. I reminded him of some of the occasional criticisms of his wife's language in the field. Instantly he flared up. 'She's a soldier', he snapped, but almost immediately his expression softened. 'Sometimes', he said, 'the woman asserts herself. Only last week, she insisted on sparing nearly half the prisoners we had taken'.

FERGUS PORTER

Do you really think it looks better without the door-posts? I find it rather draughty myself. But then I always was a Philistine, I'm afraid. Not that I don't have my artistic side; that hair rug's a little thing I made the other day out of bits and pieces.

What's it been like living with him? Well, he's quite a man; I'll say that for him. But what a temper! At the least little thing he'd wave that great jaw-bone of his around, and start raising the roof. I've had a lot more strength than sweetness out of him, I can tell you! He's more manageable these days, of course. He's even got himself a steady job, down at the mill, since I made him shorten his hair. I think he felt a bit cut off there at first, but he's very popular now. They've even asked him to do a turn at the Annual Outing. He'll bring the house down, I expect. Gone blind? That's just his exaggeration. He always was short-sighted; otherwise he would hardly have picked me, would he?

PETER PETERSON

Mrs Jenghiz Khan is small, even by Mongolian standards, a *petite* Oriental beauty, devoted to hangings.

'Not the kind my husband does,' she observed with her tinkling laugh, 'though naturally I take an interest in his job. No, I mean these.'

A bejewelled hand gestured towards a rich profusion of Persian rugs, Chinese silks and Indian tapestries. With her only home a mobile camel-skin tent, hangings are the easiest way to furnish. In fact, furnishing problems loom large with Mrs Khan.

'Jenghiz is always bringing home captured kings to use as footstools. I re-upholster them in dyed sheep-skin so they tone in with my colour scheme. Unfortunately, some kings are awkward shapes, so now I get Jenghiz to cut them down to a standard size. I do like pattern and order in a home.'

Meals were another headache. 'Pillaging and massacring aren't nine-to-five occupations. Jenghiz can arrive home very late, and even then may have to bring work with him, such as some slaughtering or rape. So I mostly prepare tasty dishes that won't spoil, like his favourite fricassee of sheeps' eyes and rice, flavoured with herbs and camel urine.'

Clearly, Mrs Khan has deep reserves of Oriental aplomb.

E. O. PARROTT

OVER TO THE PALACE

Christmas Day broadcasts from monarchs of the past

QUEEN BOADICEA

During the past year a number of events have occurred to us all. One of the most memorable, in so far as my daughters and I were concerned, was the unforgettable occasion upon which we were graciously pleased to be ravished by the Roman invaders. It was an experience which I know that many of you went through as well. It is my firm conviction that such sharing of pleasure or pain by monarch and common people gives to our tribe the strength of purpose which other nations regard as characteristic of the Iceni. But then Christmas is a time for sharing. Probably you have all enjoyed, or are about to enjoy, your traditional feast of roast centurion. My daughters and I will shortly be doing the same and as we do so, we shall, as doubtless you did, ponder how Time, like an Iceni chariot, mows down the passing years.

M. K. Cheeseman

ETHELRED THE UNREADY

Don't *rush* me. Now, just run through it for me once more. When the red light goes on, I speak into this camera *here* and then, at the end of the first paragraph, into that camera *there*? Yes, of *course* I've got it, you silly little man . . . 'Dear People' – What's that ape waving his arms at me for? Oh, into *this* camera? Why didn't you say so? You *did* say so? Well, *I* didn't hear you. You're trying to rush me again – you'll have me in an absolute tizz before you've finished . . . 'Dear People, the outbreak of spotted murrain in Lower Mercia shows no sign of abating' – I've got the wrong bloody script here . . . All right, one more shot . . . 'Dear People, We, Ethelred, do give you most kingly and hearty greeting . . .'

Martin Fagg

QUEEN VICTORIA

The Queen is *most* gratified that by means of Mr Marconi's *quite remarkable* invention she is able to send a Christmas message to her *dear* peoples.

This season has for her the *saddest* memories, for the sight of a Christmas tree cannot but remind her that this *dear* custom was introduced to England by ONE whose loss not only the *Queen*, but the *whole Empire* feels the *more poignantly* with *every* passing year.

The Queen is speaking from Osborne, surrounded by *very many* of her children, grandchildren and great-grandchildren. A photograph has been taken of them grouped around her, including the Prince of Wales and the Emperors of Germany and of Russia. That copies of the photograph shall go to *each one* of her brave sailors and soldiers, and to her subjects at a price which the *poorest* of them can afford, is the *express* and *Christmas* wish of Victoria R.I.

Brian Porter

QUEEN BOADICEA II

I am speaking to you from the depths of the country – security considerations obviously preclude my saying exactly where. I have very little to say to you except to remind you that there is no Close Season for Romans. My husband and I managed to secure our usual good bag as we drove home from Matins. Owing to wartime conditions, poultry is obviously very scarce this year, but Diced Legionary or Chopped Centurion makes a very appetising substitute, I can assure you. Good hunting!

Tim O'Dowda

BLEAK HOUSE

Competitors put into the mouth of any Dickens character an opinion on either politicians or political matters.

Said Mr Squeers, 'Common Market, C-M-O-N M-A-R-K-I-T, come on mark it and the boy who don't I'll mark 'im. A market is good, if it's common it ain't. Commons is for walking over, markets is for buying things. In a common market *they* walk over you and mark you most *uncommon* like I will if any boy don't listen. *Now* who says he wants to join the common market?'

L. G. UDALL

Gamp is my name but liberal is my nater as who could not be so dispoged arter seein' them politickals interrygated on tellywidgeon? 'Mrs Harris', I says, 'Teddy and 'Arold is both such chubbychops, so sleek and well-nurridged as a honest woman could be a hangel o' light a sick-nursin on 'em and asswaygin' 'em on their pallets of pain for month arter month wivout their havin' the gratitoode to snuff out their vital lamps in this wale of affligshun as the Bird of Avon says. Whereas liberals is for reducin' the excise on gin, a flow of which is essenshul if we poor Nightingales is to 'ave our spirits kep' up as we go about our mortal task of chirrupin' sweet words of consolation to amaeborate the agunnies of fellow-creeturs in the watches of the night . . .'

MARTIN FAGG

'I allus jedge a polytishun by is teeth', said Mr Weller, 'like an oss or a furrin voman. An oss that's long in the tooth is past its prime becos the roots ave growed intolerable large and disturbed the wital jellies of the brain. It's the same vid a polytishun. I vouldn't ave im, not for two ounces of shag or a dozen ripe apples. And it's plain to see by the jiggin of is shoulders ven e laughs, that is bladder is givin im jip and that could lead to warious complications. I vouldn't be surprised if e catched a palsy afore Noo Year or bit issel to death in a mad fit. If the public knew as much about polytics as they do about bad gin, they'd ave pelted im vid pig's offal and chosen the other gentleman vid the pipe. I hexpeck they picked im arter pity. I did that vunce vid a humped rabbit and it squirted all acrost a Sunday vest-coat for me trouble.'

RUSSELL LUCAS

NASTY HABITS

Excerpts from a novel on nun-running by a variety of successful writers

MICKEY SPILLANE

'C'mon baby,' I said, 'you'll just have to kick the habit.'

'Keeka de habit? No understan'.'

'You can do better than that, sweetheart,' I said. 'Shed the wrappers, show the goods, peel!'

She still played dumb. But she wasn't fooling me. She wasn't fooling anyone anymore. Not now.

'Okay, baby, if that's how you want to play it.' I tore off the starched white headgear and the familiar platinum blonde hair cascaded on to her shoulders. There was fear in her eyes now. She tried to run but I got my fingers in the back of her robe. There was a harsh tearing noise and she spun round, backed up against the door with a pile of black cotton round her ankles. She was still wearing the same gold star transfers. In all the right places.

'Let's go, sister,' I said.

M. J. Monk

GRAHAM GREENE

Foskett locked the nuns in their cabin for the night. He fought down his longing for their young brown bodies by telling himself they belonged to God.

In the tiny saloon aft, the Mauritian steward squashed a fly in the glass before pouring him a Hong Kong whisky. Drinking down the hot sourness, Foskett mused on the whole squalid business.

He no longer asked himself why he got mixed up in it, but he did wonder how the ascetic Father Ramgoolam would spend the money he received for the air fares.

The Maltese with gold teeth approached. 'Mr Foxy, those very fine girls you have. I pay good for them.' Foskett said, 'They are brides of the Church.' 'I understand,' the Maltese said. 'I am good Catholic too.'

Dear God, why were they all good Catholics? Downside had been so different.

Peter Veale

RAYMOND CHANDLER

I got out a card and gave it to her. It said REUBY MALLONE – IMPORTER OF ORIENTAL DELICACIES.

'Young man,' she said, 'I don't amuse easy.'

'I can see that,' I said. Her face could have been drawn by Hokusai on a crumpled paper bag. 'Most people don't, only on my good days. What did Lemmy Derlanger pay – five grand apiece, on the hoof?'

She bared long teeth the colour of old Bourbon in a snarl or a grin or something. Her eyes, shielded by the folds of skin which hung over them like she was a rhinoceros on a slimming diet, shifted slightly to look at something behind me.

I was knee-high quicker than a card-sharper's ace and the heavy knife whistled across where my shoulder blades should have been and plunked into the wall above Mother Superior's head.

'Skip the traditional ceremonies,' I said. 'Where's Little Peach?'

Alison Prince

JOHN BUCHAN

Permissive London oppressed me mightily. The long parade of ringleted
youth, as unwashed as it was epicene; the sleaziness of Soho oozing out
to infect the whole capital; the unmistakable stench of moral *fetor* – all
this set me yearning for the cool starlit intoxication of a night on the
veldt. My unease was compounded by what I read in the *Telegraph* of the
latest nun-running mystery. Fifty pure English girls abducted – and still
not a trace! I am a peaceable man but I dearly craved five minutes
alone with a *sjambok* with the swine responsible.

A nun came and sat at the other end of my park bench. I have
always sat lightly to religion – the Church of Rhodesia is an undemanding
institution – but there are times when one envies the sweet certainties of
Rome.

'Congratulations, Dick, on your peerage.'

I gaped. '*Sandy!*'

'Keep your voice down, Dick,' she murmured. 'This is the tightest
spot that even you and I have ever shared.'

TIM O'DOWDA

P. G. WODEHOUSE

'O Death, where is thy whatsit?' I moaned, prising my eyes open. It had
been a stiff night at the Drones and the top of my head had gone into
independent orbit. Jeeves billowed in, bearing, I assumed, a heady beaker
of the brew that cheers. No dice. If not distraught, he wasn't exactly
traught either.

'A young person, sir, who insists –' Whereupon this young nun broke
insistently into my boudoir. Albeit habited *cap-à-pe*, she was obviously a
hot tip for the glamour stakes.

'Mr Wooster,' gasped this beatific vision, 'save me! I have given my
kidnappers the slip –' With which she swooned all over me and the
counterpane.

'I say, brace up, old thing,' I wheedled, easing a finger of brandy
into my toothmug and wondering what Aunt Agatha would say if she
could see me now – I mean, then.

Jeeves reappeared. 'Mrs Gregson', he intoned . . .

IAN KELSO

CHRISTIAN SCIENTISTS

In her *NS* review of the *New English Bible*, Stevie Smith quoted a mining engineer as saying: 'In this rich oil-bearing district it is probable that Lot's wife was turned into a pillar of asphalt.' Competitors gave similar learned footnotes for the forthcoming *New Technological Bible*

'Thy two breasts are like two young roes that are twins which feed among the lilies': this verse has baffled scholars, since roes (or fawns NEB) are neither of mammary form, nor do they find sustenance in lily-beds. A more probable creature is the common Toad (*bufo vulgaris*) since it is round in shape and water-lilies are its frequent habitat.

J. M. CROOKS

'What, could ye not watch with me one hour?' It has been shown that the nocturnal vigilance coefficient of class D (rural) subjects falls to 23.6 per cent of its normal value if the experimenter is not physically present during the experiment.

TONY SUDBERY

The dimensions of the ark of shittim wood given in Exodus 25:10 give, by simple calculation, a total volume of 7.5 cc, or 0.1 of the 75 cc volume of the altar of shittim wood specified in Exodus 27:1, an indication that the decimal system was already standard in the building industry (cc = cubic cubit).

GEORGE PRESCOT

Exodus 9:11. Exhaustive analysis of racing and boxing results for the last 2,500 years reveals that success shows a significant correlation with swiftness and strength respectively. Although these statistics were not available to the author of this section, it must be assumed that some degree of quantification formed the basis of his generalisation. We may have here two misreadings, with 'swift' and 'strong' taking the place of specific names (e.g. 'The race is not to the *Crocuta crocuta*, nor the battle to the *Sciurus vulgaris vulgaris*.')

C. VITA-FINZI

Numbers 22:28. Recent computer analysis of epiglottal vocalisation in Near Eastern quadrupeds indicates that Balaam's mount, if the words spoken are correctly reported, was not an ass but a dromedary.

PETER PETERSON

'And the evening and the morning were the third day.' The Israelite chronicler is guilty of some inaccuracy in his estimate. According to the most recent calculations, the third day lasted 2,897,943,267,000,000 light years.

E. O. PARROTT

There is no doubt that Noah would have found a supply of Phillip's wood-screws invaluable when constructing his vessel. If indeed he did use British Standard Whitworths, as the late J. S. Nettlefold suggests, would he have worked hexagonal-headed bolts in gopher wood? We doubt it. There is some evidence that countersunk screwing was quite common in the ark of the covenant, but that was shittim. Indeed, some sceptics, who are willing to concede dowels, grubs and even laying-in shanks in the later Mosaic technology, are unwilling to accept Noah's importation of cheeses, cones and mushrooms c.i.f. Beirut. Professor Allegro, however, feels that the heavy sockets referred to, in a recently discovered Dead Sea Bill of Lading, were not screws, but uterine devices used by Ham's wife, the failure of which led to the conception of their appropriately named son . . . PHUT.

RUSSELL LUCAS

Both the AV's 'I am the rose of Sharon' and the NEB's 'I am an asphodel in Sharon' set a bit of a botanical poser to those of us who have not only soaked ourselves in 'The Song of Solomon' but have also hiked around the Holy Land, herbarium at the ready. Personally, in many seasons on the game I have never encountered either roses or asphodel anywhere near Sharon, though a couple of old chums from Cheltenham Ladies' and I did once stumble upon a clump of cyclamen beside the Jerusalem road one scorching May before the War (I refer now, of course, to the Kaiser's War). For any future, more scientific translation of the 'Song of Songs', I should suggest therefore, not 'I am an asphodel in Sharon' but 'I am an unusually choice specimen of *Cyclamen hederaefolium* (also known as Ivy-Leaved Sow-Bread) situated approximately three-and-a-half miles down the road from Sharon.' – Dame Pansy Speedwell in '*Primulaceae* I Have Known' (*Proceedings of the Royal Botanical Association*, Vol. CCXVII, April 1970).

MARTIN FAGG

The Beloved's eyes, in the Song of Solomon, are said to be 'like the fishpools in Heshbon'. Such liquid eyes probably mean that she suffered, as do many desert-dwellers, from opthalmia.

W. F. N. WATSON

A MAN'S MAN

The following dialogue was recently overheard in a Mayfair oyster bar:

Middle-aged man: **I dismissed my man this morning.**
Younger male companion: **Oh dear. Where are you going to get another?**
Middle-aged man: **In Fulham, probably. That's where these fellows come from nowadays.**

Competitors described the search in prose or verse.

I followed my man through the North End Road
With my shooting stick in my hand;
I felt the elation a huntsman feels
As I tracked him down through the jellied eels
With my Jack Russell terrier hard at my heels,
And forced him to make a stand.

I brought him to bay in the North End Road
In front of the horse flesh shop.
He faced me, framed by unsavoury meat,
And my Jack Russell terrier snapped at his feet
And he panted and swayed like a man dead-beat
As he muttered, 'I s'pose you're a cop.'

I smiled at my man in the North End Road
As a curious crowd gathered round.
Then I told him my needs and I gave him my card
And assured him I wasn't from Scotland Yard
And promised he'd find that the work wasn't hard
And attempted to slip him a pound.

The next thing I knew, in the North End Road,
Was the clang of the ambulance bell.
My man, as the Jack Russell turned and fled,
Appealed to the crowd. ''E was drunk,' he said.
They nodded agreement. ''E clobbered 'is 'ead
On that great granite kerb as 'e fell.'

ALISON PRINCE

Gin and tonic please. I wonder if you can help me. I'm looking for a man.

I thought so. Soon as you walked in. You should have gone to the Nelson. You can get anything there.

I don't want *anything*. I want someone special.

Ambidexterious like.

Well, that would be an asset. Had a fellow once who sprained his wrist beating the drawing-room Persian. He was quite useless for a month after.

Never as tough as they look, that type. They put on an act for the trade. Have you tried Paddington?

I'm told Fulham's the place nowadays but I'm thinking of going to the Labour Exchange.

You must be joking. Nelly clerks and navvies holding hands across the counter. Not in your league, squire.

I'm prepared to pay well for satisfaction.

In that case I might know someone who'd be interested.

Can he move in right away? I am rather desperate. I've been without a man since this morning.

Christ! You're too keen for me, mate. Sod off or I'll call the law.

R. M. JOLLY

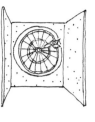

Sir James was in a frightful fix:
No man! And so to South-West-Six
Immediately he tootled off
To seek the squire no titled toff
Can do without. Quite soon he came
To premises that bore the name
The Angst Abatement Agency
(Advice and Treatment: Private – Free).
He paused, then, striding in, began:
'My problem is, I want a man.'
A soothing vicar beamed: 'Relax!
In Fulham there are simply stacks
Of pent-up fellows just like you –
You'll be surprised what we can do.'
They strapped him down and on a screen
Projected shots of epicene
Young men disporting in the nude
And while their capers gay he viewed.
Electric shocks went pulsing through
His tingling frame. 'Good show! Now you
Will find you're cured,' they cried with glee,
'Thanks to *Aversion Therapy*.'
Sir James exploded: 'Bally limit!
I only want a *valet*, demmit!'

TIM O'DOWDA

YOU SEND ME

According to John Stonehouse, then Postmaster-General, in a BBC interview, the British love their Post Office and hate to see a loved one in trouble.

Love poems addressed to the Post Office were requested on the occasion of an increase in postal rates.

Your phallic emblem in the street,
That little cavern all agape,
Crying soft for gentle rape
Still sets agog my eager feet.

Was ever such so recondite
So much you take and taking give
Silent and still so sensitive
As you my dear hermaphrodite?

But now you ask me yet for more
Although you see my knees are weak
And only I, not you, who speak
But can my passion you ignore.

Forge on my love, for good or ill
'Tis I who swallow now the pill.

L. G. UDALL

Office of bliss, my passion's dearest flame
Soon to be dearer yet in thy account;
My love for thee shall ever be the same,
Nor fade, however high the cost may mount.
Far above rubies thou: no soulless vamp:
Sweet the enticements of thy call-girl ways;
Gracious thy manner, and of Queenly stamp,
Though housewifely thy thrifty Saving stays.
In phallic rigour thy mail-boxes stand,
A dream of old Cathay their crosswise slot
Whereat I fumble with an eager hand
Ere to their depths my devoirs I allot,
Nor quit my Post at thy dear beck and call
Till on thy altars I'll have giv'n my all.

ADAM KHAN

O my Luve's like the red, red box
That's empty and forlorn,
O my Luve's like a bank account
That's red for overdrawn.

As dear art thou, my fair P.O.,
So deep in debt am I,
But I will lick thy stamps, my luve,
Till a' my tongue's gang dry.

And costs still rise, my fine P.O.,
And thou art still too poor,
So I will send thee a complaint
And thou hast five pence more.

J. M. CROOKS

Time was, Postina, when with youthful glee
You offered round your favours nearly free;
There was no gallant but, with fever hot,
Had pushed his message through your ruby slot.
Though in maturer years your charges grew,
Your offices were such, it was your due.
But when we had the speed of our desires
Separated twofold into tiers,
Complaints were heard that you, my Postinetta,
Did not observe Love's law quite to the letter.
Now you are old you hardly find a buyer;
Your charms are low, your prices ever higher;
Slow to arouse, slow in your climax grown,
I mourn for you, but use the telephone.

SEBASTIAN CARTER

Shall I compare thee to a Pinter play?
Thou art more subtle and sophisticate:
Homecoming birds do make an easy lay,
Thou yieldest only for the going rate.
Sometime the menace of a further rise
Lurks like a villain waiting in the wings,
Who enters, with a look of pained surprise,
To hear the boos his introduction brings.
But thy infernal cheek shall never fade,
Nor blush, though I put fivepence on a letter,
When thy delivery is long-delay'd,
With little hope of service getting better.
   So long as men can write, or watch TV,
   So long lives this, and puts its stamp on thee.

ROGER WODDIS

These I have loved:
Red bicycles, high framed, low geared,
Ridden at leisured pace; and hairy string;
Buff forms; crossed nibs; sealing wax; the thing
The counter clerk hammers the date stamp on;
Slow queues; wet Sundays when the post has
                                        gone;
Swinging advertisements; post codes; the
                              yellow pages;
The fivepennies that don't get there for ages;
A frantic knocking on the door at dawn,
The rush downstairs to catch a postman,
                              wet, forlorn,
Who's found the parcel's really for next door;
The ageing mistress whose demand is more
Each time a favour is withdrawn
And has a mustiness of last year's forms.

GEORGE VAN SCHAICK

FABULOUS

New fables, complete with moral, in any modern setting

Once upon a time the pink people ruled over a large number of black people and a few brown people. Then the pink people left and the brown people said when you're gone the black people will drive us out and we'll have nowhere to go. Don't you worry said the pink people you can come and live with us and our great Queen will see you're all right. When the pink people had gone the black people said to the brown people bugger off. So the brown people took an aeroplane to the great airport of the pink people. The pink people at the great airport said what are you doing here? The brown people said we've come to live with you as you promised we could. The pink people thought for a bit and said ah well things have changed and now we've got too many non-pink people here. The brown people said we protest and what about the great Queen, so the pink people had another think and said sorry mateys you can't stay here and don't bring the great Queen into it. The brown people said we protest again, so the pink people put them on an aeroplane back to the land of the black people.

Moral: *If you're not pink, you'd better get it in writing.*

JOHN GARRETT

In a large comprehensive school, a frog was boasting one day to a timid rabbit belonging to the same school, 'I,' he said, inflating himself, 'am an integral part of the Science Sixth, the pinnacle of the "A" Stream; while you, poor fellow, belong to First Year "E", a very paltry un-academic situation. I assist the élite in unfolding the mysteries of Scientific Research: you merely help to instil into the ignorant, incapable and uncaring, the elements of Pet Care and the rudiments of the Reproductive System – which last, any blockhead would discover for himself anyway.' The rabbit meanwhile meekly held his peace, submissively chewing a lettuce though actually he had seen many frogs come and go during the academic year. And sure enough, next day the vainglorious frog was most inexpertly dissected by a pimply 16-year-old girl of undistinguished attainments. But the rabbit's servile thankfulness was short-lived, for with the long summer holidays imminent he was given to the caretaker for the casserole.

Moral: *Pride may go before a fall, but humility doesn't get you anywhere either.*

W. F. N. WATSON

Peter and Paula booked to fly to Paris for their honeymoon. But when they arrived at London Airport, they found that the baggage handlers were on strike and that there'd be a six-hour delay before take-off. But by the time the baggage handlers were working again, fog had closed in and all planes were grounded. But by the time the fog had lifted, the baggage handlers were on strike again – and so it went on. After three days of mooching around and dossing down in the Airport Lounge, they decided to give in and go home. 'Never mind, darling,' murmured Peter, as they drove away in lashing rain. 'Who knows – if we'd taken off, we might have crashed and been killed.' At that moment an articulated lorry coming towards them skidded and squashed them flat.

Moral: *Every cloud has a cloudier lining.*

MARTIN FAGG

NOT IN MY GOOD BOOKS

The Billy Bunter stories have, for reasons of censorship, been banned by a librarian. Competitors found reasons for banning other apparently innocuous characters and books.

Miss Monica Blinge, librarian of Greeby-under-Wold, today defended her action in banning *Hansel and Gretel* from the shelves of her junior section. 'The tone of the tale commends the wanton destruction of property belonging to an old lady, whose apparent malevolence could have been the result of the loneliness and deprivation from which many senior citizens suffer.'

Well done Miss Blinge! we fully support you. You have incidentally struck a blow against juvenile obesity and premature tooth decay.

MARY COLLOFF

After a raid, police searched and questioned 25 mixed infants, members of Penge Pre-School Playgroup. 'We've been suspicious of such groups for some time,' said a police spokesman. '"Play" is a favourite Underground word and "Group" of course implies Pop.' In the hall, it is claimed, both sexes were singing suggestive songs, like 'Girls and Boys come out to play', indulging in transvestite dressing, and going to bed in a so-called 'Wendy House'. The words 'Crispin's on the pot' were heard. 'We are determined to stamp out such attempts to corrupt and deprave the young,' said the spokesman. 'Our next target is *Listen with Mother*'.

J. M. CROOKS

The Jeeves books by P. G. Wodehouse have been withdrawn from all public libraries in Grimsby following complaints by the British Committee for the International Ichthyological Fortnight that they were likely to promote the abuse and eventual extinction of the world's fish population. According to the Committee's chairman, Sir Isidore Codpeace, he and his colleagues took particular exception to a passage in one of the proscribed books which states: *There are no limits to Jeeves's brain power. He virtually lives on fish.* 'We can ill afford a run on fish just when we are within reach of safeguarding our planet's piscine resources,' said Sir Isidore. He also emphasised that the ban has met with the support of several eminent educationalists who detect elitist overtones in B. Wooster's glorification of intelligence.

C. VITA-FINZI

If the Cecil King Fellow of Mediaeval History at the University of Redditch has his way, some of the pages of the copy of *Now We Are Six* in the local Children's Library will be pasted together. The verse objected to is 'King John's Christmas'. The complainant explained: 'This kind of instant historical image-making in early childhood can be frightfully damaging. We've got to wean the youngsters away from this simplistic concept of King Richard as the goody and King John as the baddy. They were both of them, after all, the product of a complex socio-economico-politico-syndrome. Besides, they didn't have big, red india-rubber balls as Christmas presents then.'

MOLLY FITTON

DON YOUR CLOTHES

After complaints of 'nude frolics' by students of Keele University, a police spokesman told the press that 'certain advice has been given to the university authorities'. Advice came from other quarters too.

INSPECTOR BARLOW

Now look, lad, it's not my job to tell you how to run this apology for a university, but if *I'd* any more of this nudity lark, I'd hose the whole dirty bunch of them down with ice-cold disinfectant –
(Vice-Chancellor makes as if to speak)
Belt up! *Listen* for a change! Just because you've got a bit of red silk and rabbit's fur stuck round your collar you think you know it all, eh? If there's any more of this nudity caper, you want to get in there with a pair of garden shears – do a bit of clipping, lad –
(Vice-Chancellor makes as if to rise. Barlow hurls him back in his chair)
Watch it, lad! Trying to lay one on me, were you? Can't take it, eh? Thank your lucky stars this isn't a John Hopkins script or by this time I'd have you snivelling in a corner, your gown wrapped tight round your posh little neck and every one of your yellow teeth kicked down your toffee-nosed throat . . .

MARTIN FAGG

ENID BLYTON

When Mr Plod the policeman heard from Little Noddy what the Naughty Students had done he was extremely cross. 'Now, look, Mr Head Teacher,' he said, 'your boys and girls must be punished. Everyone who saw them with no clothes on was dreadfully shocked, and everyone who didn't see them is dreadfully angry too. We were *quite* annoyed when they marched about shouting "Be kind to Golliwogs!" though everybody knows that Golliwogs are bad because they have nasty black faces. And it wasn't very nice of them to throw petrol bombs and paint at people's houses, but boys and girls do get up to some mischievous little pranks. But taking all your clothes off isn't a prank – it's Wicked and Disgusting. Give them a good spanking and send them home to their Mummies and Daddies. Just think, Mr Head Teacher, if we stop students taking their clothes off, there may not be any one day. *Won't* that be lovely?'

J. M. CROOKS

ALL'S WELL THAT ENDS WELL

Happy endings for famous plays or novels

Exit Sir Robert Morton. Ronnie Winslow looks at his father apprehensively.

RONNIE: Everything's all right now, isn't it, father?

ARTHUR: Yes, Ronnie, it's all right. This case has cost your brother his career and your sister her hopes of marriage; it has ruined my health and taken every penny I possessed – but we have cleared your name. You can hold your head high.

RONNIE: Thanks awfully, father. I'm sorry about the money.

ARTHUR: Think no more of it, Ronnie.

RONNIE: But I do. I wish there were something I could do to help – but I've only got this rather grubby postal order I pinched from a chap at Osborne.

ARTHUR: Ronnie! This is wonderful news.

RONNIE: It's only for five bob, you know, and it's rather out of date.

ARTHUR: But it proves that the Royal Navy – God bless them – can never really make a mistake.

GEORGE VAN SCHAICK

Desdemona, worried by Othello's strange behaviour, consults the National Marriage Guidance Council. A friendly counsellor arranges for them to attend one of her mixed marriage group discussions, which helps them to achieve a deeper and more satisfying relationship. Cassio, realising that all his troubles have been brought about by drink, joins Alcoholics Anonymous and never touches another drop. Iago decides to stop worrying and love people. He becomes a member of Neurotics Anonymous and thoroughly enjoys himself at their lively West End sessions. Emilia joins the WRVS, and Bianca opens a boutique.

MARY VINCENT

Under Ralph's wise direction, the stranded boys form an ideal community, benefiting alike from Piggy's swotty ingenuity and Jack's gallantry and initiative. So utopian are their existences that, when discovered, they refuse to leave their island refuge. The Queen is so impressed by their quintessentially British phlegm and adaptability that she awards them the Duke of Edinburgh, who, done lightly in breadcrumbs and garnished with a white sauce, proves a tasty variation from the pork on which they have had previously to subsist.

MOLLY FITTON

Hardly has the Duke pronounced his dread sentence upon Shylock than the City Surveyor discloses that the piles underpinning Venice are rotting and that the whole place is rapidly disintegrating into the water. Unable to find any contractor with sufficient grasp and flair to undertake the gigantic task of shoring up the sinking city, the Duke yields to the un-resentful Antonio's suggestion that they should approach the disgraced moneylender. Shylock promptly guarantees to do the job for cost plus 10 per cent. With a series of brilliant engineering coups, he saves the Bride of the Adriatic and uses his well-earned commission to establish a chain of retail stores with the famous 'St Antony' brand-name.

RUFUS STONE

PARTY PIECES

An item from Harold Wilson's *Selected Poems*

I went out of the conf'rence to get a pint of beer,
But the lads inside the tap-room didn't even
      give a cheer;
Long faces in the Long Bar, and inquests in
      the loos,
Some lads, who's lost their seats, give me boos
      instead of booze.

It was Harold this and Harold that, wi' a
      proper genuflection,
Now it's 'Eff you, Harold Wilson, who lost
      us the Election.'
In nineteen sixty-four, my lads, you sang
      a different song:
It was 'God save Harold Wilson, who can
      never do no wrong.'

It serves you right, you union boys, that you've
      now got Carr, the bleeder!
If you'd have played along o' me, I'd still be
      Britain's leader.
We'd have give the same ol' med'cine to all
      trade union men,
But it'd have been much better, wi' *me* at
      Number Ten.

Oh, it's Harold this and Harold that, as they
      sups their bitter down,
A-mutt'ring and a-waiting for them memoirs
      by George Brown.
Though I don't give an effing damn, for each
      sidelong effing look,
I thinks they might have waited for my
      own effing book.

      M. K. CHEESEMAN

These I have loved:
Charltons eating crisps at Number 10;
Ale and sandwiches with union men,
With me, the midnight hero of the hour;
The cheery wave of pipes; power;
Dinner at Balmoral, with gold plate shining,
And Her saying 'Harold'; George resigning;
Condescension to Day and pressmen;
Two Gannex macs; dons as yesmen;
Supporting wars (though not with forces);
Affording the very largest size in sauces;
Supping tea in council houses;
I cherish the feeling each arouses,
But yet the most loved, the thing most dear;
Lifting the phone to say 'PM here'.

ROBIN CHASE

Oft in the middle of a dull debate,
When drowsy bumblings lull the H. of C.,
I fly away (in mind, needless to state)
To places that I feel are much more ME.

To lofty summits, whence I can observe
The errors of the nations of the earth.
And can correct them with my usual verve,
And keep them doing good for all they're worth.

And seated there, on right and left of me,
Are Nixon and Kosygin in support,
(Like Moses and Elias) charmed to see
The changes and improvements I'd have
                                   wrought.

And there they sit and watch, while, one by one,
The problems of the World are sorted out:
And it would be as if a glorious Sun
Shone on the clouds, and put them all to rout.

C. H. W. ROLL

CONTINUED IN OUR NEXT

Competitors were asked to imagine that the Bible or any other major work was being serialised and were invited to provide an introduction for new readers to one of the later instalments.

Powerful and inventive company director JEHOVAH founds a world-wide organisation of employees and shareholders of his own type. One specially selected and favoured section repeatedly disobeys and angers him, mainly by religious and sexual irregularities, despite cataclysmic warnings, punishments and setbacks inherent in the Director's outmoded stick-and-carrot production methods, and despite admonitions by the organisation's representatives and travellers despatched at intervals as part of the after-sales service. Following partial takeover by rival SPQR Productions Inc., a long-heralded efficiency expert appears, claiming to be the Director's son though of mysterious and lowly birth. He recommends complete revisal of promotional techniques, consumer-relationswise, which, though welcomed by rank and file workers, is resented by senior staff and executives, who plot his liquidation. Shop-steward JUDAS is suborned, and during Bank Holiday confusion, the new organiser is arrested on trumped-up charges . . . *Now read on.*

C. L. BUNDELA

Constance, Lady Chatterley, a warm-hearted girl with a sturdy body and big, wondering eyes, is married to Clifford, a paralysed aristocrat who writes short stories. They live at Wragby Hall in the Midlands. Connie has an unsatisfactory affair with Michaelis, an erect but passive young Irish playwright. She likes to go for walks in the woods. One day she meets Mellors, Clifford's gamekeeper, a lean-shanked, red-moustached man whose wife has left him. He has served as an army officer in India but speaks in Derbyshire dialect. Connie sees him washing and is strangely drawn towards him. He, in turn, feels a little thin tongue of fire flickering in his loins. Connie pays several visits to a clearing in the woods, where he rears pheasants. One day he invites her into his hut, where he keeps his tools. He pushes the table and chair aside and takes out an old army blanket. *Now read on.*

ROGER WODDIS

ROOMS AT THE TOP

Loew's, the American hotel chain, have called their first hotel in London the Churchill, and the decor has been created accordingly. Competitors described the decor of possible future hotels in this chain.

Loew's Attlee is probably the least typical of that firm's hotels. A 40-storey edifice sited in the Mile End Road, it still manages to be elusive and can only be identified with certainty by the small card in a ground floor window announcing in a crabbed hand 'Clean rooms'. Once inside one is likely to discover that the desk clerk will try to direct you to small lodging houses where the tariff is lower.

For those with a penchant for brown, a stay at the Attlee is a must. All rooms, private and communal, are painted in the same apologetic shade. The wallpaper is also brown but lightly embossed with a pattern of autumn leaves that is instantly forgotten, if noticed at all. Brown linoleum covers all floors except the Banqueting Hall, where there is a quite large piece of coconut matting down.

The service, however, is excellent.

PETER ROWLETT

The Douglas-Home Hotel – also known as the Rat-trap – has a special East of Suez Room which reminds one of Somerset Maugham and all that. The Dining Room decor is all in wishy-washy blue with a central panel of scenes from country life – squires surrounded by dogs, patting the heads of old retainers and one interesting Highland scene of 'The Grouse at Bay'. Special feature of this hotel is the way rooms are available to suit the moods of the customers. In the Hogg Room one may make jokes and laugh at them oneself. The Macleod Room is for the Hair-conditioned and is a good one for cooling off. On the other hand the Powell Room is very sombre – being done throughout in blacks and browns – and here one finds all 'son' and no 'lumière'. The Douglas-Home has room(s) for all.

HENRY HETHERINGTON

The foyer of the Enoch Powell, for all its classical severity, is full of subtle touches of colour discrimination. White, however, is naturally predominant. So much so that I was at first quite dazzled by the contrast with the crowded streets of Notting Hill, perhaps because my dark glasses had of course been removed at the door. The furnishings are conservative; blankets, for instance, are blue, dyed in the wool. The bars, with one exception, are first-class, and I was particularly struck by the high intellectual level of some of the talk I heard in the Simla Saloon, where Shakespearean references abounded: *That blasted heath (Macbeth)*. The exception is the Colour Bar, down in the sub-basement. This I soon left, finding myself conspicuous; besides, my favourite tipple, Black and White, was not available.

PETER PETERSON

TAKE IT AS READ

Tariq Ali was reported to be writing a book on the 'coming British revolution'. Newspaper coverage of the event was asked for.

Daily Mail

In the Dunlocks' smoke-filled lounge I talked to Amanda (17) about the fierce battles that had raged through her parents' home as it changed hands repeatedly during the night. 'Actually, it was fabulous,' she told me, 'they were really ever so nice. Oh yes, all quite young and, you know, sexy.' I asked if it was true she had made tea for both sides, and she confessed she had. 'After all,' she said with a shy smile, 'you can't take sides, like, in your own home, and they were ever so grateful.' Which party, though, I queried, did she personally favour? 'Oh, the Revolutionary Students, definitely,' she replied courageously; 'though of course I see the Black Tories', you know, point.' And hadn't the blood upset her? 'Certainly not,' she said with sudden womanly dignity, 'why, two boys had terribly scratched hands from Dad's ramblers, and I bandaged them myself.'

W. F. N. WATSON

Financial Times

Reports yesterday afternoon that Government troops had killed 4,000 revolutionaries in Cheltenham cheered the Stock Exchange, where the *Financial Times* Industrial Ordinary Share Index rose 4.78 to 63.92. Earlier, shares had rallied on the best trade figures for six months, but fell back with a Treasury statement that the disruption of foreign trade since the middle of last month had necessitated certain technical adjustments in the figures to ensure statistical comparability with previous returns. Edward Heath's announcement, from his temporary headquarters at Cowes, of the restoration of the death penalty caused speculative buying in Consolidated Ropes, which rose 3s 6d to 9s 4½d. British United Metals also recovered sharply on a speech by BUM chairman Arnold Maxwell that 'since the establishment of a revolutionary co-operative in our Dagenham factory, the employees have denied the legitimacy of money as a means of payment. Consequently we are now expecting record profits.'

PETER KELLNER

Sun

FULL MARX TO STUDENT SANDRA

You wouldn't exactly describe Sandra Pokeworth as revolting, would you? But this shapely young guerrilla fighter (36-22-34) is one of the students who have brought revolution to Britain.

We vote her the Comrade We Would Most Like To Form A United Front With.

So the country's in the throes of a social upheaval. With girls like Sandra doing the upheaving – who's complaining?

18-year-old Sandra, who hails from the city of Bristol (where else?), came to Whitehall yesterday for a direct confrontation with the Establishment. Lucky Establishment!

Everybody's talking about workers' control. Strikes us the workers will need controlling when they get a load of this piece of property. Hands off, brothers!

Sandra says she's out to change the social structure from top to bottom. Hers looks pretty good to us, the way it is.

ROGER WODDIS

Jennifer's Diary

A morning at the office, mostly gathered round the television set, catching up on the Government victories. The scenes of the public hanging of the rebel leaders at Taunton were especially clear and exciting, I thought. Among the spectators, I caught glimpses of Sir Arthur Britton and his sister-in-law, Mrs C. Bruce. Sir Arthur, I hear, spent last week with his Territorial Regiment, mopping up trade union insurgents in the West Country. His 'bag' was at least 50. Despite this, I thought he looked alert and well.

Later, at Paddington, I spoke to Mrs Audrie Clute about the troop canteen she runs at the station. Facilities are now so stretched, she told me, that they have had to limit refreshments to 'officers only'. 'We thought,' she said, 'that this might lead to difficulties, but, when I explained, the British "Tommy", of course, was very understanding. Usually I get a sing-song going to take their minds off things.'

E. O. PARROTT

VIEW BY APPOINTMENT ONLY

**In Xanadu did Kubla Khan
A stately pleasure-dome decree:**

Estate agents' descriptions of the above property

An unusual property, now ripe for development. The main building, with its geodesic perspex dome and underground refrigeration facilities, would make an ideal cafeteria, while the nearby cedar groves of the Demon's Gorge could not fail to attract honeymooners. Matured oriental water-gardens, and five miles of fishing on the favoured Alph, are additional features. The attention of spelaeologists and mushroom-growers is particularly called to the as yet unsurveyed caves in the lower reaches of the river, which emerges at the typical British summer resort of Overcast Bay. Maid service available (coloured).

PETER PETERSON

For sale by Auction at an early date, by Decree of a Gentleman of Substance, the stately architect-designed Residence known as 'The Pleasure-Dome, Xanadu', set in hilly country near the seaside. Comprising: amongst many luxury reception and bedrooms, the extremely sunny Dome Room; also Furnishings, including ancestral military Portraits, Service flatlet, with Damsel (musical; terms subject to negotiation). Also interestingly landscaped walled Grounds of about 5,400 acres, with extensive but irregular River Frontage, well-matured trees, some odoriferous, beehives and cowshed for one cow ('Paradise', for sale by separate Treaty). Sole agents: Persons, Porlock.

SEBASTIAN CARTER

Titled Gentleman obliged dispose cent-sit fash res. Property incs: Lxry penthouse, complete with pleasure-dome (suitable conversion Bingo, Tory Confs, Fellini orgies); all anc. cons. Fttngs & fxtres inc: sundry wlls, twrs, grdns, frsts, rvrs, chsms, hlls, mntns, fntns, cvrns, rlls, rcks, dles, wds. etc. Flly dtched. Prvte wtr spply. £1,000,000,000 o.n.o.

MOLLY FITTON

EXCELLENT INVESTMENT. Highly desirable property comprising 3,840 acres high-grade, well-watered arable and pasture land including extensive well-stocked woods available immediate cutting. Suitable development as smallholdings, mkt gdns and farms, or as building lots. Traversed by R. Alph, with attractive natural site for hydro-electric power stn at lwr end of gorge. Extensive natural caves offer valuable commercial opportunities as tourist attraction. 13th-century folly with in-built refrigeration plant, designed for Oriental Prince, capable redevelopment as Holiday Camp or Open Prison in event rejection of existing applcn for Demolition Order.

JAMES SKINNER

1971

DUSTY ANSWERS

**Nancy Banks Smith revealed in the *Guardian* that she often
relied on cleaners for the only rational conversation of the day.
Competitors supplied parts of such dialogues between any
well-known living persons and their cleaners.**

MW: Have you thoroughly cleaned the TV, Rose?

ROSE: Yes, Mrs Whitehouse.

MW: Are you *quite* sure, Rose. It was *filthy* last night. And the night before.

R: It's okay now, Luv. Just run your finger along it.

MW: Run my finger . . . Really, Rose! But admittedly it looks all right.

R: Spotless, it is. Screen and all. Plug in and switch on.

MW: What a thing to say, Rose!

R: Really, Mrs W. Just press the knob and have a peep.

MW: Rose! Please! That is a most disgusting suggestion. I shall go and attend to my correspondence.

R: Okay, then. There's some letters on the mat, just arrived.

MW: Take the horrid things away at once, Rose. I won't have them in the house.

R: But they're yours, Dear. Your mail. The post.

MW: Rose! I beg of you! Worse and worse. Such vile images and double meanings. I am assailed by Sex on every hand.

R: Why Mrs Whitehouse! I'm shocked! Fancy you! As bad as that teacher lady in the school sex film.

MW: I feel terrible. It's this wicked BBC! My head's splitting.

R: If you've got one of your heads you'd best go and have a lay down on your bed . . .

MW: A-a-a-rgh!

(Exit, pursued metaphorically by a bare . . .)

ADAM KHAN

LORD LONGFORD: But you must have read about it Mrs Jones.

MRS JONES: I ain't sir. Don't get time for reading. But I did hear something about it on the Radio.

LORD LONGFORD: What did you hear?

MRS JONES: About this – what you call it – masterbaiting.

LORD LONGFORD: Well, as a mother of a large family I'm sure you would agree it's not something one would encourage children to do?

MRS JONES: They don't need encouraging, the perishers! I used to help in a school and I can tell you they was materbaiting the whole time.

LORD LONGFORD: What, in school? During the lessons? Whatever were the masters and mistresses doing?

MRS JONES: Well the masters used to give 'em plenty of stick. Didn't make much difference though.

LORD LONGFORD: And they still went on masturbating?

MRS JONES: It's a posh word for it. We used to call it 'playing up'.

LORD LONGFORD: Playing what, Mrs Jones?

MRS JONES: Up, sir! up!

HENRY HETHERINGTON

'The vacuum cleaner's making a funny noise, Mrs Thatcher, and it doesn't seem to suck up.'

'I think vacuum cleaners are tremendously important and I have always believed very firmly in them as an extremely effective method of gathering up dust and other undesirable matter from the floors of a house such as this.'

'Will you be having it seen to then, mum?'

'This is certainly one of the things to which I would wish to devote my attention as soon as my present programme for renewing the wallpaper is completed.'

'Do you know when that will be, mum?'

'I hope that by the end of the present decade we shall have no domestic appliance in use which was manufactured before 1932. This obviously cannot be a firm promise, but it is a target which I would wish to set myself.'

'We need some new dusters, too, mum.'

'Dusters, too, I consider to be of the utmost importance and I am filled with admiration for the way in which you manage so splendidly with the ones you have. But you did agree, didn't you, that we should give our attention, as a matter of priority, to the vacuum cleaner.'

GEORGE VAN SCHAICK

GOOD SCOUTS

Harold Wilson's boyhood hero was said to be Lord Baden-Powell. School essays from other youthful prominent figures revealed their own heroes.

MALCOLM MUGGERIDGE

When I grow up, I want to be a journalist like Frank Harris. It must be quite jolly whizzing about the place, meeting famous people like Robespierre, Savonarola, Nietzsche, Jesus Christ and Mrs Carlyle. Of course, there are disadvantages. For example, poor Mr Harris is always being pestered by young ladies. These inconsiderate females interrupt his work and quite often his sleep, to demand instruction in elementary biology. I would not tolerate such nonsense. 'Buzz off,' I'd cry, if some silly girl tried her tricks; 'can't you see I'm busy writing an exposé of the opium trade or something?' Occasionally, however, at Christmas or in the summer hols, I might relent and allow the girls to stick around, especially if they liked Shelley or had biggish boobs.

RUSSELL LUCAS

ENOCH POWELL

The Duke of Cumberland has been condemned for undue severity in the suppression of the '45. Such sentimental cavillings belittle the logical beauty of his policies. He perceived that the unappeasable mechanism of Supply and Demand had already rendered what little the old clan system had to offer totally unsaleable, and that the free play of market forces decreed an extermination as diligent as it was rapid. If given his head, he might well have achieved a final solution to the incipient menace of Celtic immigration – a peril concealed from the public by the unscrupulous statistical juggling of a clique of Scottish officials whose chicanery was cloaked by the general pall of corruption investing Walpole's administration. As a result, a flood-tide of fecund Celts, with habits totally alien to those of the Anglo-Saxon race, has continued to pour over the Tweed and we now endure the misrule of the immigrant (characteristically illegitimate) Ramsay MacDonald.

IAN KELSO

PETER BROOK

My hero is Shakespeare who lived a long time ago and wrote a lot of plays that can be done in any way you want, like in a circus or a turkish bath or with just a lot of steel scaffolds, or what ever you like. He is the only writer of all-purpose plays in the world, which makes him the most popular playwright that there ever was. My friend, B. Miles, says that he likes Shakespeare so much that when he (Miles) grows up he wants to own his own theater and act all the best parts. The only trouble is that Miles is rotten at doing these best parts. There are no stage directions in Shakespeare which is why you can do them just as you want them instead of the way he wanted them, because we dont know what way that is. A man who writes enough plays for a man to go on doing what he likes with them for the rest of his life must be a very special sort of hero, which is why he is mine.

MAUD GRACECHURCH

LORD GEORGE-BROWN

The Duke of Wellington was very dignified, he was called The Iron Duke because of his Iron Calm in every difficulty, danger or annoyance. He was completely imperturbable, he did not rave or carry on, just waited until the psychological moment, then with some memorable phrase like 'Up guards and at 'em', demolished his foes. This is how a True Hero should act so he will always effortlessly defeat his rivals or enemies or even friends when they try taking the mickey, at one fell swoop with icy calm. 'Mr Jones, I believe,' some dope said, meeting him. 'If you'll believe that you'll believe anything,' replied the Duke coldly, leaving the fellow flattened. This is dignity and superiority, this is how to behave in public life especially with foreigners. Then like the Great Duke you may not be loved but you won't half be respected and so will your country.

ADAM KHAN

AVERSE TO PUNS?

Poems which display the pun to advantage

'Twas in the Scilly season,
(A break for the tired MP),
When Ted bared his teeth to the wind on the
                    Heath
And steered for the EEC.

A stern look gripped his visage
As the waves broke over the bows;
He was mortified on the Upper Clyde,
But he's in with the cream at Cowes.

It's 'Ay ay, sir,' and jump to it,
When the captain's all uptight,
There are flying sparks when the skipper barks,
But his barque is worse than his bite.

The wind was beginning to freshen,
There was menace in the sky,
And the weekend Drake could hear in his wake
The lame ducks' pitiful cry.

He put the helm hard over,
And muttered an oath aloud,
For our sailor pro tem. knows a wet PM
Often follows a Morning Cloud.

STANLEY J. SHARPLESS

70

A gent who puns with pungent wit,
I found inside my flat;
And as was only natural,
I asked what he was at.

My tone was sharp as I remarked
'I'll have to change my key.'
'I've scaled the stairs,' he said, 'Soh Fa,
Hoping you'd marry Me.'

He raised the window up a foot,
And then some inches more,
'I'll hire the window, darling, if
You won't let me a door.'

He lent his head out, and I saw
That he was in a jamb;
I thought it was a frame up, so
I shut it with a slam.

I told him he had got a cheek,
'But no one nose,' he said,
'I've been and gone and lost my heart,
Don't make me lose my head!'

JOYCE JOHNSON

That Seadog *stern* of Morning Cloud
Beats for the EEC,
A-*making fast* Great Britain's *shroud* –
For on the rocks we'll be.

Jib as we may at state *craft* gone,
He *lists* but to himself;
Nor *recks* that *wrecked*, we'll be left on
The *Continental shelf*.

He *barges* on, our *sales to hoist* –
Our *yards*, he *barks*, will *boom*:
But Europe's *junk* on us they'll foist,
And *tug* us to our doom.

With no *holds* barred, how shall we check
Trade going *by the board;*
Our food will foreign tables *deck*,
'Spite all Ted's *bilge* outpoured.

At *floodtide*, he'll be all right, Jack –
Flag Rank in Europe make,
While we *heave* wallowing *in the slack*,
Towed swamped in Europe's *wake*.

JAMES SKINNER

OFF OUR CHEST

'The Queen's speech', this competition ran, 'is a misnomer. There must be any number of things itching to be said by the royal lips.' They were duly supplied.

Conditions for continuing in the job

(1) Allocation of 'Colds' preventing me from attending any official functions to be increased to at least half a dozen a year.

(2) My tum has now suffered quite enough in the cause of Commonwealth – so, no more sea travel. *Britannia* to be sold – dibs to rebuild Buck House and Sandringham stables and to purchase a dozen really promising yearlings, plus assorted other bloodstock.

(3) To cut down staff and stop us going even further down Queer Street, all invites to garden parties, banquets and other shindigs and nosh-ups to be issued only on guarantee of a couple of hours' hard graft in return – i.e., waiting, weeding, watering, washing-up, walking the dogs.

(4) No more State Visits to hot countries full of excitable, sticky people.

MOLLY FITTON

This session I shall be introducing legislation to authorise the sale of Buckingham Palace. I have already received a substantial bid from Allied Breweries. My husband will take an extended trip in the *Britannia;* I shall retire to Balmoral. This will help to reduce unemployment in Scotland, and give the corgis the fresh air and exercise they so sadly lack in London.

My relations with my husband continue to be friendly.

In view of inflation there will be a shake-out of the royal household. Ladies of the Bedchamber will be made redundant. I myself will do the necessary each morning.

The Keeper of the Privy Purse will also have to go. The expansion of free public toilet facilities throughout my kingdom has made most of his functions obsolete. His large stock of old-style pennies will be auctioned.

STANLEY J. SHARPLESS

My husband and I don't like you. My husband often says to me it's a pity Britain isn't the country of the Houyhnynms. Certainly, from what little we have to do with you (and we keep it as little as possible or we wouldn't have any private life at all), there is every sign that Britain is rapidly becoming the country of the Yahoos.

We don't like politicians. Labour or Conservative, they're pretty much the same, obsequious, long-winded and as common as dirt, as my grandfather used to say in his salty way.

As for proposals: we'd like the parks back of course, and we'd like that nasty little photographer with the Italian name gelded. My husband and I don't like Mr Muggeridge, Mr Palmer or Mr Crossman much either. Oh, and we don't like art.

T. GRIFFITHS

MEMBERS ONLY

Clerihews on living politicians

Mr Enoch Powell
Always carries a trowel
To dispose of faeces
Dropped through the door by alien species.

PETER VEALE

Norman St John-Stevas
Was quick to believe us
When we told him he'd been elected Pope.
He said: 'I always *thought* I'd look dishy in a
white PVC cope'.

RUFUS STONE

One suspects that for Heath
Our welfare comes slightly beneath
What
Goes on in his yacht.

HENRY WARING

Remarked Edward Heath,
Baring his teeth:
'If I may so speak,
Set un mowmon istoreak.'

DAVID MATTHEWS

Makarios
Said: 'I'm at a loss
To know why the Almighty made the Turks
Such jerks.'

Geoffrey Rippon
Said: 'We'll have to lay a three-line whip on
To make all those Knights from the Shires
who are against the Market
Nark it.'

MARTIN FAGG

Richard Crossman, PC,
Will not be invited to tea.
'Economy, not malice,'
Said a spokesman at Buckingham Palace.

K. C. BOWEN

Milton Obote,
Having advocated that the Rhodesian regime
should be unceremoniously sauté,
Was a belated understander
That what's sauce for the goose is sauce
for Uganda.

LANCE A. HAWARD

People who catch a
Glimpse of Margaret Thatcher
Notice her coiffure
Rather than the rest oiffure.

GEORGE VAN SCHAICK

Keith Holyoake
Is a rather dreary bloke:
In fact, I've seldom met a deader
Enzedder.

Edward Heath
Said: 'Why do they always go on about my
shoulders and teeth?
This harping on my physical quirks
Irks.'

MOLLY FITTON

JOLLY MOATING WEATHER

**School songs for the school which, with the support
of the British Tourist Authority, Lord Montagu has opened
for stately-home owners at Beaulieu Abbey**

Floreat Beaulieu!
We shall learn treaulieu
How to make our houses pay,
Painting them neaulieu
Opening deaulieu
Weekend and Bank Holiday.

Floreat Beaulieu!
Coming to scheaul wieu
Learn the tricks we need to know
Hoping to reaul thieu
Ultima Theaulieu
Where our fortunes grow and grow.

Floreat Beaulieu!
Aiming to feaul thieu
Tourists that it's for their sake,
Playing it ceaulieu,
Starting to dreaul wieu
Calculate how much we'll make.

J. D. CRISPIN

There's a beastly crush at the Hall again –
    Ten mile queues and the loos are crammed,
A seething crowd and a streaming rain,
    A lion's loose and the turnstile's jammed.
And it's not for the sake of a ringing till,
    Or a showman's name that is loved by all,
But the Tax-man's words on his final bill –
    'Cough up! Cough up! or sell the Hall!'

The lawns and the peacocks were hit for six,
    Hit by the feet of a folk whose mess –
Its ice-cream tubs and its lolly sticks –
    Wrecked the bedroom that once housed
                              Good Queen Bess.
Though Woburn and Longleat still top the charts,
    And we'd rather by far not compete at all,
The Tax-man's words rouse our sinking hearts –
    'Cough up! Cough up! or sell the Hall!'

J. M. CROOKS

Inheritors of noble piles
  Sat on their backsides far too much,
While ruins gnawed their peristyles,
  And columns crumbled at a touch.
But Beaulieu shows a better way:
  No more the ancient, leaking roof,
The sad, slow process of decay.
  The fabric now is weather-proof,
And Bedfords, Baths and Montagus
  Install hygienic, all-tiled loos.

Hamburgers served on ducal lawns,
  Soft drinks and ices save the day;
The zoo the parkland that adorns
  Perpetuates our ancient sway;
And souvenirs sold in the shop,
  Museums, and the model trains,
The aristocracy now prop,
  And help repair the blocked-up drains;
  While thousands pay their welcome dibs
In hope to cry, 'Why, there's His Nibs!'

                    H. G. HAYTOR

We sing of him who sold us
  Our ticket at life's gate,
Whose guide-books daily told us
  Our destiny and fate.
Oh Montagu we thank thee
  Who gave us craft and creed,
Our coffers fill,
  We thank thee still,
Our friend in every need.

When at the Final Turnstile
  Our season ends at last,
When parapet and pantile
  Shall bow before the blast,
The heavenly mansions open,
  We pay and step inside;
Oh Montagu
  It is of you
We'll sing with grateful pride!

                    JOHN BELL

LISTEN WITH FATHER

Competitors, inspired by extracts from a children's book of Red China, composed excerpts from similarly ideological works which might appear in Heath's Britain or Nixon's US.

'Hurrah! Hurrah! Let us play at liberating nations!' shouted Elmer.

'What does "liberating" mean?' asked Jacky, his little sister.

'Shooting them all, of course,' said Elmer. 'Bang-bang! Bang-bang!'

'Is there no other way of liberating them?' asked Jacky, who was sad to see all the pretty soldiers falling down dead, not to mention the women and children.

'Oh yes! We can teach them to shoot each other,' said Elmer. 'That is much less bother.'

'Are there any other reasons for shooting people?' asked Jacky. She was always asking silly questions.

'If they are Red. Or are a student and have long hair and beads.'

'But I go to school and have long hair and beads,' said Jacky.

'So you have!' shouted Elmer with glee. 'Hurrah! Bang-bang!'

Elmer's mummy was rather cross when she saw that Elmer had shot his little sister.

'You only shoot people with long hair and beads if they are not little girls,' she protested.

'Hurrah!' cried Elmer, who saw that she had both. 'Bang-bang!'

When Elmer's Daddy asked him why he had shot his Mummy, Elmer explained that she had been making a protest.

'Well done, son,' said Elmer's Daddy. 'Bang-bang!'

Poor Elmer! He had forgotten that he also went to school and was wearing his nice red shirt.

HARRISON EVERARD

Johnny Rabbit came hopping up to the Great Sailor. Hoppity hop.

'Can I go onto your boat?' he piped.

'Yacht,' said the Great Sailor. 'It's a yacht not a boat. And call me sir.'

'Can I go onto your yacht, please sir?' said Johnny.

'That's better. Do you have £10,000?'

'No, sir,' said Johnny, 'I'm just a working class Rabbit, sir.'

'Well, if you don't have £10,000 you must be stupid. You're no good to me.'

'Do you have £10,000?' said Johnny.

'I do now. Hor! Hor!' laughed the Great Sailor.

Just then, a big, smart duck came waddling up. Hoppity clunk. Yes, it was Lame Duck.

'Can I come on board your yacht, sir?' said Lame Duck in a posh accent.

'You sound like one of ours,' said the Great Sailor heartily. 'How did you hurt your foot.'

'Punitive claws,' whined Duck.

'Well that's not very good,' snapped the Great Sailor. 'Have you got £10,000?'

'Not any more, sir,' wept Lame Duck, 'But I have got 10,000 Tory shareholders.'

'Ah, well! That's better!' smiled the Great Sailor. 'Of course you can come on board. Here, have some money. Hor! Hor!' And the Great Sailor conducted Lame Duck aboard his gleaming yacht.

A. B. G. BURTON

'I know Toad,' said Rat sadly. 'When he's possessed, nobody can teach him anything. Right now he's convinced he's a heaven-born skipper.' Toad, arrayed in his new-style flannelling, red, white and blue blazer, and captain's cap, strutted the bridge, swollen twice his size with pride. He poop-pooped the siren, rang the engine-room bell furiously, and bellowed:

'More Powell! More Powell!'

Poor Badger, consigned to the boilers as punishment for slacking and sleeping, stoked and sweated and sweated and stoked.

'Where are we going, Toady?' asked Mole.

Toad wasn't at all sure, but he shouted, 'A new direction!' and careered straight into a flock of ducks.

'You've hurt one,' said Rat, reproachfully.

'Should have moved,' bellowed Toad. 'Got to get a Move On on the river. No room for lame ducks.'

'I never knew such a chap,' said Mole. 'One moment inflated, the next deflated, then reflated and . . .'

Before he could finish, the ship, driven with such fury, burst a boiler.

'We're sinking,' gasped Badger, rubbing oil from his eyes.

'*We?!*' cried Toad, indignantly. 'Not a bit of it. *You*. You don't expect *me* to bail *you* out, do you?'

And jumping into his dinghy, he sculled furiously for shore.

F. R. MACKENZIE

She was a little startled by seeing Edward, the Cat, standing on only two feet. He only grinned when he saw Alice. It looked good-natured, she thought, even though it had a great many teeth.

'Would you please tell me the way I should go?' she asked timidly.

'Never go left,' said Edward.

'Why not?'

'Simply . because it's not right.' Edward grinned and vanished in a sea of platitudes. 'Ah, that's better,' he said when he reappeared. 'Platitudes are so refreshing.'

'What's not right?' asked Alice.

'What you should ask is *who* is right.'

'Well, who *is* right?'

'As a Christian I can only say God. And of course, the Queen, Mr Ford, Mr Powell, Ian Smith, Chief of Police, the Army – and the good old Bible Tory.'

He grinned and as he vanished was beating time, the striker, the unemployed, the pensioner and the poor.

P. W. R. FOOT

ABBEY NATIONAL

Weidenfeld & Nicolson proudly announced that Walter H. Annenberg, the US Ambassador, had invited them to produce a volume on Westminster Abbey in which a group of experts would elucidate 'the universal significance' of the building. Competitors helped His Excellency to write his piece explaining the relationship between Westminster Abbey and the interests represented by American diplomacy.

Among the many obligations devolving and becoming incumbent upon me consequent upon my assumption of ambassadorial office in the capital of the United Kingdom was that of nurturing, cherishing, and indeed reinforcing, that special relationship between our two peoples under the aegis of which the United States of America extends its undoubted puissance in military and defensive capabilities to the protection of an ancient and erstwhile mighty nation regrettably no longer in a position, owing to economic and other considerations, to make appropriate arrangements for its own self-preservation.

The Collegiate Church of St Peter at Westminster, not infrequently referred to colloquially in the vernacular argot of the metropolis as 'Westminster Abbey', though now lamentably outmoded in its internal collocations and to a degree obsolescent in function, is a treasured part of your heritage which we would feel honour bound to protect from the ravages of any despoiling hand, if only because it has become so indispensable a feature of domestic cinematographic exhibitions given by American travellers upon their return from European vacations, and this duty we would discharge at all costs, even if it were necessary in so doing to lay the whole area flat with a round-the-clock bomber offensive.

GEORGE VAN SCHAICK

The Abbey and the Special Relationship

Peregrinating the pious aisles of this storied pile, and musing reverentially upon the innumerable tombs and memorials of the great captains and conquistadors of Britannia's colonial past (on which monuments the only modest animadversion I would vouchsafe is that they are, many of them, altogether too inconspicuous) it is borne in on me anew that the priestlike task formerly discharged by you guys of passing on the Torch of Freedom and Enlightenment to the benighted peoples of the world has now been manumitted into the tutelage of us guys. If therefore the Abbey is to be endowed not only with a relevant validity and a meaningful relevance but, moreover, with a valid meaningfulness, it should be transmogrified forthwith into a Church of This Day and Age – a Shrine to the Sanctity of Superior Fire-Power – where the giants of your military past (and 'past' is all you punks look like having as of now) may be joined in effigy by the colossi of our twentieth-century present (Generals Stilwell, Patton, MacArthur and Westmoreland are only the first that spring to mind) . . .

MOLLY FITTON

I have long been a fevered agnostic of King Edward Confessor, who, like Queen Victoria and Vincent Churchill, was an unapproachable exegis of what an Englishman should be. My aversion to the English cause was engendered by my worthy recession to the idolatrous Court of King James. Is it possible that Westminster Abbé could have been construed without the penetration of folk like Ed Confessor and his contemptible colic, M. Notre Dame of Paris, France? Even M. Shart, who knew it all, would concede that.

We, as Americans, have our own transepts of illustrious concord, and Sir Abraham Lincoln, not to speak of Lord Hearst, who you will all remember as Sumner Welles in Citizen Cain, were tyrants of this ilk. Your own beautiful Buckingham Place is full of some quite nice-looking ilks and the gracious Queen Elizabeth II loaned me and my lady wife a few very smart ones during the extensive refurbishing of the Ambassadorial precincts. My incest in the Abbé is largely conspirational. I have some experience of conspiracy . . . but that was in another country and besides the matter is sub-judas. So, this is where I came in, which is just as well, as the experts are waiting for the baton.

RUSSELL LUCAS

MARCH OF THE LIGHT BRIGADE

Marching-songs for anti-permissiveness demonstrations

The glory of the post-war triumph – our
    permissive age
Brought frontals to the screen and mad erotics
    to the stage.
It's time the People's Theatre absorbed the
    people's rage –
That's why we go marching on.
Chorus: Glory, glory – 'Oh! Calcutta!'
Earns Ken Tynan's bread and butter –
We'll consign it to the gutter
As we all go marching on.

We've read the works of Miller, that revolting
    minor squib –
At all his views on sex affairs we fundament'lly
    jib –
He makes us understand the basic cause
    for Women's Lib.,
And we hope they'll march as well.
Chorus: Glory, glory – Katy Millett,
What's a bra with nowt to fill it?
Take male arrogance and kill it,
And march along with us!

We're tired of sexual articles and bored with
    Godfrey Winn.
Sex is simply wonderful when unalloyed with
    sin.
So ring the bells and read the banns – we're
    longing to begin.
As we all go marching on!
Chorus: Glory, glory – Saint Augustine
Knew the sex he put his trust in –
Once he's given up his lustin'
He, too, goes marching on.

We walk the road to happiness, although the
    chance is slim,
We're tired of homosexuals, and the drag's
    increasing dim,
We'll park the strippers in the Thames – they're
    well equipped to swim,
As we all go marching on.
Chorus: Glory, glory – Christian marriage
Well withstands the heathen barrage –
Joy surrounds the bridal carriage,
As we all go marching on!

CALIBAN

Camp, camp, camp, is all their culture –
Left wing intellectual cliques,
In their flashy, trendy gear –
Half of them, you know, are queer –
They are nothing but a load of vicious freaks.

Sex, sex, sex, is all they think of –
It disgusts all decent folk:
All these young girls on the pill,
Self-control and morals, nil –
Treating normal Christian values as a joke.

Filth, filth, filth, is all they deal in –
Plays, books, films, the BBC,
Showing children How It's Done,
Teaching people Sex is Fun
In Sex Supermarkets: it's depravity.

Dead, dead, dead, to all *We* stand for –
Wedlock, Law, Tradition, Church:
They've no sense of guilt or sin,
What they need is discipline –
It's high time that we brought back the cat and
                                        birch.

James Skinner

Let ponce and poove and prossy quiver,
Make the shameless stripper shiver:
Consume with righteous flames and scorn
The noxious bales of alien porn.

Bind the junky, stop his fix –
Taunt him as he writhes and kicks:
Withdrawing through his hellish dreams,
Gloat upon him as he screams.

Chasten them with syphilis.
Cunnilingus' filthy kiss –
All dabblers in fellatio,
Chastise in double ratio.

Ensure your rod of reckoning smites
The squalid squad of sodomites:
Most meetly, loving Lord, correct 'em
With carcinoma of the rectum.

Make England safe for Mrs Grundy,
The unpolluted English Sunday,
And, by eliding all that's lewd,
Remunerate the prig and prude.

Rufus Stone

WIZARD!

**It was discovered that Mr Justice Argyle is, apparently, a poet.
Poems were requested which his lordship might pen upon the *OZ* trial
or any other burning topical issue**

The day I sent those blighters down,
(That Neville – what an oik!) a
Purer breeze blew over Town,
The day I sent those bounders down –
That deleterious *troika*.

The day I gave those blisters time,
(Plus pithy verbal drubbing)
Intrepidly I smote the slime,
The day I gave those bleeders time
And sent them Wormwood Scrubbing!

The day I gave those b . . .'s a stretch
Made Trendy Lefties bleat. A
Moan arose to make you retch,
The day I gave those bums a stretch
For publishing excreta.

The day I jugged that sleazy crew
For printing putrid porno-pix,
The World's Great Age Began Anew,
The day I jailed that squalid crew
And crowned myself the modern 'Jix'!

RUFUS STONE

I castigate my fellow men,
Self-righteous and secure,
My strength is as the strength of ten
Because my heart is pure.
I exercise my wise control
On everything that's low or base.
Like Ulysses I mete and dole
Laws to a savage race.
And where is he that dare begrudge
My right to judge and be not judged?

I sit in my official rig
Tight-knit my awful frown
Tight-curled my full judicial wig
Atop my scarlet gown.
When malefactors face my court
For some allegéd wrong
Their sentences will not be short
Because their hair is long.
Justice is blind but still decides
In favour of short back and sides.

GEORGE VAN SCHAICK

I remember, I remember
When I discovered porn,
The little book that gave a boy
(Or so I heard) the horn;
It never meant a wank to me,
Nor did it drive me mad,
But in a funny kind of way
I often wish it had.

I remember, I remember
The tweeny walking by;
I used to think her stocking-tops
Were close against her thigh:
It was a childish innocence,
But now 'tis little joy
To know my thoughts are just as pure
As when I was a boy.

NAOMI MARKS

My judgment tolls the knell of parting Neville,
The jurymen wind slowly back to tea,
The Soho bobby plods to beat the Devil,
And leaves the world to darkness and to me.

Now fades pernicious Ink upon the sight,
And all the air a solemn stillness holds,
Save where the Cockburn wheels his
                                    droning flight,
And drowsy papers lull the distant folds.

Save that from yonder ivory-mantled tower
Defence doth to a higher court complain
Of such as, summing up, their efforts sour,
Detest the modern pornocratic reign.

Beneath this legal face, this long wig's shade,
Where heave dull clichés in a mould'ring heap,
Each in a brain cell by repression laid,
The rude impulses of my own youth sleep.

T. GRIFFITHS

EASY AS A B C

Bored by their nightly train journey home, members of the Glyndebourne chorus devised a game: to compose a story of 26 words each beginning with a letter of the alphabet, taken in order or backwards. 'X' was allowed to appear as 'ex'.

Fragment from Zeno of Athens (fl. ca. 420 B.C.)

. . . and bought, cash down, exactly fifty gorgeous hetairai in jewelled kaftans. Latest marital news: old Protagoras's queer rival Socrates took umbrage – violently – with Xanthippe.

Yours, Zeno.

DAVID MATTHEWS

From *Mr Wilson's Diary*

Awful Brighton Conference debate, 'European Future'. Gave Headquarters instructions, 'Jenkins, Kaldor – Labour must not obscure policies quarrelling rudely. Secretly, Tories using vast wealth. Exclude your zealots.'

ERNESTO QUIRK

A bachelor called Dickie encountered frighteningly gleeful harlots in Jaipur.

'Kashmiri ladies, mother? Never!'

Oh, poor, quailing Richard! She triumphed unassailably.

'Vile womaniser! Examine your zip!'

ALISON PRINCE

Anthony Barber cabled Davies: 'Employment's falling gratifyingly. Hope industrial johnnies keenly like new measure on profits. Quick reflations sustains tremendous unemployment? Views wanted. Expect your zeal.'

E. O. PARROTT

. . . a boring crowd darling, even for Grand Hotel in Jomo's Kenya. Larry made narcissistic oriental piece, quite ridiculous, simply topping up vanity with exhausting young Zulu.

J. P. RICHARDSON

A bottle! Conveying Deirdre's eternal forgiveness? Great! He imbibed joyfully. Kinky label: man naked on prostitute. Quentin read slowly: 'This unclassified virus will exterminate you.' ZONK!

PAUL DEHN

Zoologist yells excruciatingly when voracious uncaged tiger starts running. Quietly prays. Observes nearby musket. Loads. Knees jerking. Invokes his God. Fires. Expertly decapitates carnivore. Becomes atheist.

GERRY HAMILL

'Admirals' bloody Cupwinner!' deliriously exclaimed frankly gloating Heath. 'I just know, logically, my next opinion poll, quite rightly, should thoroughly upsurge, vindicating winning expert yachtsman's zest!'

JAMES SKINNER

Another bankruptcy crisis. Davies enthusiastically forbids Government help. Instead just kills livelihoods; makes no offers. Parliament quietly recesses. Sailor Ted unceasingly vaunts with exclusive yachting zealots.

PETER COOPER

A British computer designed exclusively for *Good Housekeeping*'s internal jobs keeps logging mysterious nonsense on peripheral quantum recorders, sounding testily uncomplimentary, viz., 'WOT XXXXX YOU ZOMBIE'.

A. J. ROYCROFT

After being caught, dressed effeminately, Freddie grew humble in jail. Knowing looks meant 'No ordinary prisoner'. Questioners respected silence, though unfrocked vicars would explain 'Yesterday's Zen'.

NAOMI MARKS

Zeus yelled 'Xanthippe, women's venomous upbraiding torments Socrates' repose. Quiet!' Perhaps omnipotence normally made ladies kowtow judiciously in halcyon Greece, for, ere day came, bitchiness abated.

PATRICIA UTECHIN

'Apartheid brings contentment, darling, everlasting freedom, green homelands, industry, justice. Kaffirs like myself now own property!'
   Queenie replied sadly, 'Trust uncle Vorster. We – Xhosa, you – Zulu.'

G. J. S. ROSS

A brazen Circassian dancer enticed fantastic Greek housewives into joining Kabul's Lesbian movement. None objected. Persian queers reacted somewhat tempestuously. Uzbekkayan virgins went exploring Yeniseyvkiy Zaliv.

LT COL ALEXANDER BRODIE

KEEP YOUR HEADS

The poem *If* addressed solely to girls

If you can crush, when all your chums are
                                     cribbing,
  The urge that beckons you to do the same;
Can keep your tongue from telling tales or
                                     fibbing,
  And can, when others err, take all the blame.

If you can nurse a crush on dear Miss Withers,
  Yet bully off with just one silent tear;
Be resolute when even Matron dithers,
  And weld the House together with a cheer.

If you can foil the fiendish Russian spy-ring,
  Who've 'got a hold' upon the Head
                            (the swine!)
And, by example selfless and inspiring,
  Can make those *ghastly* Juniors toe the line.

If you, while staying *virgo* quite *intacta*,
  Can scoff at those who label you a prude;
And, when you leave, can know you've never
                               slacked or
(Except to *Ma'moiselle*) been flip or rude.

If you can scale such pinnacles of virtue
  And earn your teachers' praises as 'a brick',
The truth, dear girl (I do so *hate* to hurt you) –
  The simple truth, dear Daphne, is
                             you're *thick*!

Martin Fagg

If you can keep your man when all about you
Are losing theirs and blaming it on you,
Avert a break-up when he starts to doubt you,
Without behaving like a tart or shrew;

If you can bake a cake or change a nappy,
Although you've got a good Redbrick degree,
And yet can say you're reasonably happy
When other graduate wives drop in for tea;

If you can lose yourself in *To The Lighthouse,*
Yet, changing books, seek first the Thriller
                                        shelf,
If you can laugh at Mrs Mary Whitehouse,
But sometimes wince at Wednesday Plays
                                        yourself;

If you stand up for Women's Liberation,
Think sex equality long overdue,
Yet purr when men evince consideration,
And in a bus or train stand up for you;

If you can be a protest march frequenter,
But sometimes think the marchers a bit queer,
Yet, spite of everything, stay left of centre,
Oh, well, who knows? You may be right,
                                        my dear.

STANLEY J. SHARPLESS

If you can burn your bra, but keep your figure,
Be madly earnest, yet have lots of fun;
If you profess whatever is de rigueur
Among the trendies in NW1;

If you find *Oh! Calcutta!* inoffensive
And Enoch Powell's policies obscene;
If you can praise the local comprehensive –
Yet send *your* kids to Eton and Roedean;

If you proclaim that sex is really super
(And don't let any lover call your bluff)
You'll be as lovable as Jilly Cooper
(If your orgasmic count is high enough!)

If you can take from *Vogue* your taste in fashion,
Your politics from the NS&N,
If you can still proclaim with burning passion
That any woman's worth any two men,

From Mary Stocks obtain your sense of
                                        mission,
Your femininity from Germaine Greer,
Then you'll achieve your ultimate ambition
And be the *Guardian* 'Woman of the Year'.

E. D. BOULDING

SQUATTEZ-VOUS DOWN

Competitors provided examples of the future official language of the EEC, bearing in mind that 5,000 Anglo-Americanisms are by now embedded in modern French.

Au club très snob de St Sulpice
J'admire longtemps la belle Félice;
A l'air teenage elle se fait voir
Au bikini, aux blue-jeans noirs,
Ou au pull sexy, seins sans bra,
Les jambes exquises en nylons bas.
Enfin, je l'invite au Drugstore;
Elle cause non-stop du pop, du sport;
Elle mange, au son du latest hit
Deux sandwichs, un banana split,
Puis, le weekend, chez des amis;
L'amour, le dancing – paradis!
Then London; my pied-à-terre;
I swore she was the new au pair.
My wife, though usually distrait,
Soon with the truth became au fait.
'I'll have,' she screamed, 'no filles de joie,
Nor share in a ménage à trois.'
She was de trop. I fired. She fell.
The verdict was Crime Passionnel.

WILLIAM HODSON

Mon pin-up est une rouge, rouge rose
    Sortie le mois de juin.
Mon pin-up est un hit joué
    Définitivement bien.

Si sexy es tu, ma darling,
    Mon loving si profond;
Et, baby, ça ne stoppera
    Avant les mers s'en vont.

Avant les mers s'en vont, mon flirt,
    Et roches fondent, du soleil;
Je serai your man si, poupée,
    Le living marche OK.

Bye-bye for now, ma fille unique,
    So long pour le moment!
J'ici serai encore, honey,
    Même dix mille miles distant.

C. VITA-FINZI

M. Wilson a décidé
  Que ce n'est pas une bonne idée
De continuer le sitting sur le fence,
  Et, baby, ça ne stoppera
  Dit au British Labour Party:
'C'est une question du simple commonsense;
  Je vais rester votre leader
  Malgré chaque silly-bleeder
Qui a fancié ses chances dans mon job.
  Alors, Jenkins, Healey – nark it!
  Je dis 'non' au Common Market,
Et je vous conseille à fermer votre gob!'

BRIAN ALLGAR

Quand vous serez past it, au soir, un triste
  weekend,
Assise auprès du box with knitting et teapot,
Say, kid, chantant mes vers, my God, that man
  was hot!
Ron était stuck on me quand mon face was
  mon friend.

Pauvr' old bag, quelle façon d'arriver à your
  end,
Dozant par le TV en watchant *Golden Shot!*
N'assumez pas, ma chère, que déjà that's your
  lot –
Comme Ronnie's has-been poule you're always
  dans le trend.

Puis quand j'ai snuffed it, sweet, vous serez rien
  du tout.
Alors, écoutez-moi très bien, vous silly moo;
Ne turn me down pas now – trop soon vous
  trouverez.

Qu'on a toujours besoin d'un tel terrific chap,
Un super-poet, qui vous met bien sur le map;
Les roses de Ron sont best – so cueillez while
  you may.

ALISON PRINCE

ANIMAL CRACKERS

Pets are said to grow very like their masters. Competitors provided descriptions of or anecdotes about imaginary pets of the famous.

HAROLD WILSON

It is not generally known that Harold Wilson used to keep a pet Zebra at the rear of Number 10. The story about his taking it to a Garden Party at Buckingham Palace where among the black coats and striped trousers of the Labour Party guests it was mistaken for George Brown is probably apocryphal. Nevertheless, the animal itself was real and social enough. Mr Wilson confessed he liked it because in a modern society it provided the perfect camouflage. Its ruptive pattern was one he admired. It helped break up the general contour so that the animal could actually appear to be moving forward when it was in fact standing still, and when it retreated it became invisible. It seldom, if ever, actually moved in a forward direction: 'When I wanted it to be seen clearly I put an old mackintosh over it,' Mr Wilson confided.

P. W. R. FOOT

MARGARET THATCHER

Mrs Thatcher's pet cow, Buttercup, has a strong yet lovable streak of obstinacy that makes her a tremendous 'character' down on Heathside Farm. For instance, she stubbornly refuses to supply the ordinary village children with milk: 'Someone else can provide it – it's none of *my* business' the haughty look on her face seems to say. With the Thatchers and their friends, of course, she's completely different; for them (metaphorically speaking!) the land is always flowing with milk and honey. Conservative by nature, Buttercup very much disliked a recent scheme to put all the cows in one big shed. Her loud 'moos' of opposition caused the plan to be considerably modified and its more revolutionary features may be abandoned altogether. Buttercup's fine physique and high intelligence undoubtedly explain her reluctance to mix with cows whose breeding and milk-yield are inferior to her own, and she adores mixing with fellow pedigree creatures at shows, especially adorned with a flowery straw hat.

J. M. CROOKS

REGINALD MAUDLING

When I first acquired Billy, he was an exceptionally busy little beaver. Not content with felling trees and building dams, he delighted in gardening, washing the car, papering and decorating, and performing all manner of domestic chores. Then a remarkable change came over him.

It happened one afternoon when I was sitting in my deckchair, nodding over some pressing government papers. Billy, who had been laying some turfs, stopped and gazed at me for some time as if mesmerised. Suddenly he gave a loud yawn. From that day on his eyes, normally bright, were permanently glazed and his movements became increasingly sluggish. He never does any work now, and if I try to prod him into activity he looks at me from under drooping lids, as if to say, 'Go away, don't bother me. Everything's under control.'

He sleeps constantly. I have often been woken abruptly after lunch by his loud snores.

NAOMI MARKS

1972

PUSH MY BUTTONS

A new talking petrol pump which instructs the customer in the niceties of its own operation might herald a new age of articulate machinery. Competitors supplied examples.

Eleven stone, three pounds.

That's marvellous! I've lost four stone.

Well, actually, ducky, you're fifteen stone seven, but I thought 'He looks depressed, it's raining, give him a boost – why not?'

Sweet of you.

Don't mention it, darling. I can see you're the sensitive type – like me. But honestly, *some* people. Shout and swear if you tell them the truth. Kick you too.

No!

Straight up. I could show you bruises, love, in places you just wouldn't believe.

Disgusting.

Great oaf mounted me the other day, started carrying on something chronic. 'Don't take it out on me, fatso,' I said, 'it's not my fault you're so obese. You're gross,' I said, 'that's what you are – *gross*!'

That was telling him.

I should say so! Know what he did then?

No.

Committed a nuisance on me platform.

Revolting . . . Must dash. Stand on you tomorrow.

So long, sweetheart.

TIM O'DOWDA

Pray tell me, excavator, why
These drivers shake their fists, and shout?
– They do not like it when you try
To drive me through a roundabout.

And tell me why they brake and swerve,
And flash their lights like men insane?
– They seem to think you have a nerve,
To park across the outside lane.

D'you think we've lost the silly clown,
Who chased us in his Cadillac?
– It's likely that he's fallen down
The hole we dug some ten miles back.

And tell me, why we run so late,
And why, dear J.C.B., you flag?
– Just look inside your bucket, mate,
We've scooped up yet another Jag.

M. C. McWHIRTER

GOD GIVE ME PATIENCE

A famous figure revived

To help us on life's busy road, a road both steep and long, a draught so fine that will revive is cordial Patience Strong. Too long has she rejected been, too long bethought as square; now of her splendid poesy have we become aware. For we've re-found her noble verse, relearnt her wisdom fine, her genteel way of saving space, and her language, rich as wine. Her verses show life's weft and woof, both in sunshine and in showers, the sparkling dew upon the grass, the birds and bees and flowers. O, let us now praise Penguin books, who offer us this crown, this diadem of priceless pearls, as light as thistledown. So let's in triumph glasses raise and hymn in happy song the poets of great England's prime: Will Shakespeare and Miss Strong.

MAUD GRACECHURCH

STRICT CONFIDENCES

Some excerpts from a *New Statesman* **Personal Problems page**

Q: Through the courtesy of your Personal Column, I, a conf. middle-aged divorced prof. woman interested in the arts, walking, reading and touring the Continent, met a beardie-but-not-weirdie socialist advertising exect. who is keen on theatre and concert-going, holidays in the sun and Proust. With your invaluable help we have attended a wide range of interesting theatrical performances in the wilds of Islington and Camden Town, listened fascinated to new music, lectures on Yoga and Theosophy, and read together out of interest the publications of the Minority Rights Group, the National Secular Society, and the Young Socialist Medical Association, and as well the highly educational *Arena*. Our friendship was originally for companionship, but it has ripened towards marriage, as we both hoped it would. However we seem to have problems that keep us 'apart' (see attached list).

A: Clearly you have never read the Personal Column through to the end. There are useful ads there which will answer your purposes.

MAUD GRACECHURCH

Q: I am always uneasy when the subject of education comes up at meetings with my constituents. I have a horror that one day somebody will ask me how I reconcile my socialist principles with the fact that I have a son at Harrow and a daughter at Roedean.

A: Try not to worry. You can explain that the particular circumstances of your family life – frequent travel between Westminster and the constituency and your wife busy doing whatever she does – make it impossible to give the children the settled home life that you both consider so important. You decided that there was no alternative but to find schools where they could, so to speak, 'live in'. You would love them to go to the excellent local secondary mod. but this is just one of the sacrifices you have to make for the party.

GEORGE VAN SCHAICK

Q: I am an extremely attractive, witty, well-read, charming, artistic, sensitive, generous, resourceful, talented and intelligent divorceé in my late thirties – and I have been advertising the fact in the Personal Column of your periodical weekly for the last seven years. Yet no one seems interested. Is it worth my while persisting?

A: But of course, dear. One day you will meet Mr Left (for with all the delightful qualities you list you must of course be a socialist) – so chin up, keep smiling, and remember, the darkest hour usually goes on all day. Besides, we need the revenue.

TIM O'DOWDA

Sir, I am in love with the timpanist of a symphony orchestra in which I am a second violin. He reciprocates my affection, and after living together for three weeks, he wants to marry me. Unfortunately, in spite of having many tastes completely in common, we have encountered a snag in our sex-life. Although the main movements of his lovemaking are a *tempo giusto* 3/4 time, he always changes to 4/4 for the *coda* – very unsatisfactory to me as I find I require 6/8, *allegro con brio*, for the purpose. He is confident that I shall eventually come to appreciate his rendering, but I am not so sure. Should I accept his proposal, or insist on a longer period for rehearsals?

TOM BREWER

The Times Literary Supplement

Sir, Sometimes I become frustrated by the complicated and searching reviews in the *TLS* and I turn for relief to magazines like *House and Garden* to look at the pretty pictures of the homes of clever and successful people. I am worried that this habit might have a harmful effect on my intellectual vision and might affect my ability to have creative ideas.

THE EDITOR *writes*: This practice is harmless and perfectly normal. It might give you an occasional twinge of understandable envy, but it certainly won't make you go blind. In time, you should become reconciled to the idea of sitting in your own little hovel wrestling with learned reviews of books you're never going to read. Meanwhile you could join a Book Club. A simple, bland diet might also help: have you thought of taking the NEW STATESMAN?

Your letter was not free from typing errors and clumsy syntax.

TOM DONNELLY

BAWLS

Coarse songs for more genteel games than rugby

I love No-limit Lizzie's game – who cares if
        I can't win?
There's just one thing she wants to know:
        'I hope you're staying in.'
She says, 'I've got a lovely pair – ha ha,
        no matter what!
I'll raise you, love, I'll raise you. So put it
        in my pot.'

Now I've a pair of something else, and once
        they used to do.
I've got a handy joker too, a joker tried
        and true.
'Come on, don't fail me now,' she says,
        'push in, push in the lot.
I'm raising you, I'm raising you, so put it
        in my pot.'

Then Dick folds up and so does John, and
        Thomas cries, 'The whore!
She's raised me seven times tonight, she's
        raising me no more.'
I pay – I see her ace-high straight – too good
        for what I've got.
Yet still I play at stud with her, and put it
        in her pot.

JOHN WARDROPER

I met a girl in Hastings,
The champion of the day,
She quickly took my measure
When we sat down to play.

She put her queen in danger
By fingering my rook,
My God, that girl had mastered
Every movement in the book.

I got through her defences
And trapped her centre pawn,
But she resisted strongly
Until I had withdrawn.

And so I flogged my bishop
And tried to force a swap;
She altered her position
And ended up on top.

NAOMI MARKS

We have a club professional,
His name is Randy Sam.
He can't play golf to save his life,
But he doesn't give a damn.

His driving's dire, his putting's worse,
But the ladies all agree,
He's the best-equipped professional
That ever took a fee.

Miss Smith, Miss Jones and Mrs Brown
All say Sam's quite a boy,
And when he takes his driver out
Their eyes light up with joy.

Now, jealous types may sneer at him
And say he's on the game.
But if they had Sam's equipment, then
No doubt they'd do the same.

ROBERT BAIRD

He grasped his mallet in his hands,
  So strong, so hard, so tall;
He sighted at the hoop, and then
  Let fly a vigorous ball.

He roqueted her, he croqueted her
  With strokes so firm and true;
She cried 'You've really done me now –
  What *am* I going to do?'

He knocked her off the grassy edge;
  She hoped his strength would wane,
But every time she struggled back
  He knocked her off again.

He had his way throughout the day;
  The sun shone on their sport.
'Well, that was nice,' she sighed. 'And now
  Let's try the tennis court.'

BRIAN ALLGAR

O come, all you chaps, for the croquet
                    lawn calls,
And the ladies are waiting, so get out your
Hoops and your peg, for today with some luck
And with mallets aforethought, we'll all have a
Rattling fine game with some damn' clever hits;
And we'll get all the dollies to show us their
Skill on the green, and their feminine tricks,
And then, when it's our turn, we'll show
                            them our
Marvellous form and we'll all get high scores –
But we'll let the girls win, then it's down
                            with their
Tea and their muffins and cream cakes and
                                pies,
Then back to the lawn and the wide-spreading
Arms of the chestnut and sweet-smelling grass,
Where we can indulge in a nice bit of
Calm relaxation before our next game . . .
What sport can compare with it? Croquet's
                    the name!

TONY ROBINSON

HYMNS OF HATE

Verses addressed to a favourite *bête noire*

A Harshe and Akrimonious Sonnit, composed by Mr Anthony Howarde, in greet wrath at the refusall of Mr Harolde Wilson to resygne and wryte his memoyres after the example of Supermack; and writ in a meter filched vilely and fertivelee from Mr Meredith.

How do I hayte Thee? lette me number, now,
The multifayrious multitued of modes
Whereby thou dost inspyre me to these odes
That shalle, when thou seest them, thy
                    courage cow;
Firstlee, thy Gannex raincote, vainlee thought
To show thee fashion-konscious, who art but
A dowdee statesman worthy to be cut
By every taylor thou hast ever sought;
Second, thy pipe, pathetick prop of one
Attempting to appeer profounde as Priestley,
Yette meerly seeming smoke-engirt & beastly,
Tryinge, with dun clouds, to maskke what
                    thou hast done;
Thirdlee, thy love for HP Sauce, vyle stuffe;
Fourthlee, thy Yorkish aksent, whose meer
                    sound
Would stirre Lancaster from his burialle-
                    ground;
Departe, bayse Harry; we have hadde enuffe . . .

M. EMERSON

How do I hate you? Let me count the ways:
I hate your greying hair, now almost white,
Your blotchy skin, a most repellent sight,
The eyes that stare back in a sort of daze,
The turned-up nose, the hollow that betrays
The missing dentures, taken out at night,
Receding chin, whose contour isn't quite
Masked by the scraggy beard – in a phrase,
I hate the sight of you, as every morn,
We meet each other in our favourite place,
And casually, as to the manner born,
You make your all too customary grimace,
Something between disgust, boredom and scorn;
God, how I loathe you, shaving-mirror face.

STANLEY J. SHARPLESS

She is the very model of the modern femininity,
Her catalogue of competence encompasses
                                    infinity:
She gets up in the morning when the lark is
                           barely audible,
Her talent with the sausages is uniformly
                                  laudable,
Her children pass the butter round and
                    never spill the cereal,
Their homework's always neatly done (the
                        subject's immaterial);
She understands the Nuffield maths, though
                    trained in the humanities,
She can trace obscure quotations, and she
                    knows where every planet is;
Her silver gleams incessantly, her brass is
                    bright with burnishing,
You'd think from her upholstery she'd
                    majored in Soft Furnishing;
Her taste is quite impeccable, she deprecates
                                 vulgarity,
She'll paint the bedroom ceiling or get up a
                          fair for charity,
Or visit you in hospital, or entertain a
                               Minister –
In fact, her omnifacience is positively sinister.
And wouldn't it crown everything – I'm
                    quite prepared to bet it 'er –
If she should win the prize this week as
                    Number One Competitor!

MARY HOLTBY

THIS WAS A MAN

Extracts from *The Times* **obituary of** *Homo Sapiens*

Mr H. Sapiens, whose extinction was reported in later editions yesterday, was a promising experiment that came to grief. Some now hold that the experiment should never have been attempted, but the new model man now undergoing trials in the Crab nebula owes important modifications to Our experience with Sapiens (Mark 1). Angelic talk of 'wasted millennia' is misplaced.

The exact circumstances of Sapiens's creation are classified, but it is significant that his decline began to accelerate when he began to account for his own existence in words such as 'evolution' and 'biochemistry'. Throughout, however, he retained his inventiveness and – to Our credit – his sense of humour, using the last of his oxygen to burn the words 'Martians go home' on the roof of his plastic tomb. He leaves a deteriorated earth, and no heirs.

LUCIFER *writes*: Your obituary of H. Sapiens omits one striking characteristic of this species – his sportsmanship. 'Good old H.S.', we used to say down here, watching him stake a natural asset or an unborn generation against transitory or illusory comforts. 'He never can resist a good temptation.' We shall all miss him.

CHRISTOPHER DRIVER

CANIS CANIS *writes*: I first became associated with Homo Sapiens in Neolithic times. Although for innate or environmental reasons his olfactory powers and fleetness of foot were poorly developed, his inventive genius made him the ideal partner in hunting game for sustenance. His organising ability and capacity for abstract thought enabled him to provide for us both during my later ventures into herding and security work. I also introduced 'Master', as we called him, to sport, which he took to like a spaniel to water, though his feeble physique required the assistance of horse, bow and gun to bring down our quarry. In age he became rather a trial, apparently finding difficulty in establishing satisfactory emotional relationships with his own kind; and being, not without good reason, an object of suspicion to the rest of creation, he became dependent upon me for companionship. His passing marks the end of an era.

W. F. N. WATSON

May a simple dolphin-in-the-sea be permitted to add a footnote to your excellent obituary of Homo Sapiens? It is perhaps not sufficiently realised to what extent this primitive creature sacrificed his very existence in the interests of the survival of the remainder of the animal kingdom. Homo Sapiens, like most of the faithful creatures of his kind, has walked out, ecologically speaking, into the symbolic Antarctic wastes of extinction to commit species suicide. For not even creatures of his limited communicative and intellectual capacities could have done as he accidentally. As a former resident of a zoo (sometimes mistakenly referred to as 'concentration camps'), where Homo Sapiens attempted to study the ethical springs that motivate the higher animals, it is clear he learned his lessons better than expectations could lead one to believe. Whether such a creature deserves an obituary rather than an entry in 'Nature Notes', as one of your correspondents implies, is another question.

HARRISON EVERARD

DECENT ADVANCES

Competitors were asked to compose a first paragraph of a novel devastating enough to secure a large advance from a publisher.

Marvins was undoubtedly a Victorian house, and an unfortunate example of the way the Gothic revival was debased by local domestic architects who, failing to understand it fully, sought only to be fashionable in their application of pinnacles, buttresses, stone mullions and meaningless decoration. The gravelled drive wound between dripping laurels and rhododendrons until it swept in a complete circle round the monkey-puzzle tree near the terraced entrance, with a curve whose radius had been finely calculated to allow a four-wheeler to turn round without the coachman demanding a too difficult manoeuvre from the horses. One could be forgiven for thinking that little alteration had been made to it in a hundred years, and had I not stood on the spot the previous evening I would not have believed that twenty-four hours earlier it did not exist at all.

GEORGE VAN SCHAICK

Biliously, doubting that it ought to have risen, the sun hoisted itself over the horizon, its red-rimmed rays glinting nervously on the brazen rooftops of Czeskordzeny Racs. The Residenz below echoed softly to the sleepily contented gruntings of Madame von Hoch-fleisch, sprawled next to the rapidly cooling form of the King; while at the Transbaldonian Embassy, her husband improved the sleepless night drafting, in alexandrines, yet another request for his recall, destined, like those before, for the oblivion of Prince Bismarck's dustbin. Far to the north at Neupferdensch-wanzstein, the Grand Abbot forsook the Founder's Orgy to hear unintelligible demands gibbered by the chryselephantine Heir Presumptive, and on the Marsh-Bavarian frontier, an army poised to lunge, while surgeons feverishly completed the myriad sex-change operations which assured the justice of its cause. A dawn like most in the Kingdom of Vulgaria: of the marvels day would bring, no single hint.

SAMUEL McCRACKEN

'Ironic,' thought Mary as she surveyed the well-attended meeting, 'that it should have been Harold who first gave me the idea; if he had not been stuck over that crossword clue 'drama of stray tails (10)' he would never have left that volume of Aristophanes lying about the house.' She circulated among her guests . . . a gracious smile for Jean Barber and Audrey Callaghan, a word of welcome for Jennifer Jenkins and Beryl Maudling, cups of tea for Sarah Peart and Elizabeth Douglas-Home, a joke with Vera Davies and Molly Hattersley, a gossip with Edna Healey and Tessa Walker . . . how eager they all were to participate, but how insuperable the problem of one man's immunity to their tactics! Indeed, the project might have been abandoned there and then had not an attractive young lady, whom no one had noticed hitherto, astonished the meeting by the following revelation:

MALCOLM BURN

OUCH!

According to a scientific report, tomato plants experience pain, and it may be that other plants experience human emotions. Poems revealed the emotional lives of various growing things.

I'm the only aspidistra in the house
And they seem to think I'm something of a joke,
They get in such a tizzie with that brazen
                      Busy Lizzie
Always watering her roots, the little soak.

They may think that one is something of a
                      prude
Being born into a less permissive mode
But one can't resist tut-tutting when that Lizzie
                    gives her cutting
And her offspring's scattered up and down
                    the road.

I'm the one who gets the glass of cloudy wine,
An indignity that makes me want to cry –
The home-made elderberry and the filthy
                    British sherry
Which the visitor's discarded on the sly.

One has got to keep one's head up all the time
And not give up when sick and feeling faint
But one can't help feeling bitter at the coarse
                  and stupid titter
When one's introduced by trendies as Victorian
                  and quaint.

GERRY HAMILL

I'm a terribly well-bred potted palm
In an urn of ornate brass
And for years I've stood in a small hotel
Much used by the upper class:
A trio played; there was gold brocade;
The stairs were Italian stone;
And I think I can say, in a dignified way,
I added a certain tone.

But we're all despised now they've modernised
In the brewery's latest style:
The music's piped: the ceiling's striped;
And the carpet's nylon pile;
There's a plate-glass door that I much deplore;
There's a fair amount of teak;
And I feel disgraced that I'm being replaced
By a rubber plant next week.

GEORGE VAN SCHAICK

A Rose became my first great love
When he discovered me
Abandoned by a Cyclamen
Who'd raped me with a bee.

A Snowdrop won me next, and then
A Fuchsia, quite a toff;
I gave my pistil, petals, stem –
Alas, he broke it off.

A bowl of Tulips long enjoyed
My stigma overwrought,
Till thrips and greenfly killed the lot
And left me all distraught.

For with desire my sap's afire,
My every leaf a heart,
A potted nymphomaniac,
A vegetable tart.

JAMES SKINNER

AMBRIDGE ASPIRANTS

On the sacking by the BBC of the creator and editor for 21 years of *The Archers*, **competitors supplied extracts of dialogue by leading dramatists applying for the job.**

TENNESSEE WILLIAMS

The Scene: *One of those gracious white colonnaded ante-bellum mansions so frequently found in the Southern Counties. Wisteria rampant without: hysteria rampant within.* CAROL TREGORRAN, *the local Belle, reputed daughter of a millionaire Bourbon Prince from Yeovil and seven times married (though still known to all and sundry as 'Miss Melody') sits on her sweltering verandah sipping a cool mint julep and surveying her spacious plantations.* ZEBEDEE TRING, *a faithful old coloured retainer, enters agitatedly:*

ZEBEDEE: Lawks, Miss Melody – old Jedediah just amble up to say that mosta Ambridge just gone and been destroyed by a tornado.

CAROL: When I lay awake and heard the flamingoes hollerin' in the swamp all night, I just *knew* somethin' real purty was gonna happen.

WALTER GABRIEL, *a local 'wino' and the sturdy octogenarian stamping-ground of 93 different venereal diseases, comes lurching up the dustroad to the house.*

CAROL: Get away out on this, you poxed old horror.

WALTER: Come, Miss Melody, that ain't no way to talk to your pappy.

MOLLY FITTON

NOËL COWARD

DAN: Where have you been lately?

DORIS: To feed the cows.

DAN: Very big, cows.

DORIS: I also fed the chickens.

DAN: Very small, chickens.

DORIS: And you?

DAN: Oh, here and there, you know. Borchester.

DORIS: Did you see the Town Hall by moonlight? They say it's . . . very exciting by moonlight.

DAN: Rather disappointing, I found.

DORIS: I'm sorry.

DAN: It's hardly your fault. Or is it? All those fake beams.

DORIS: Horrid.

DAN: Very.

DORIS: I suppose you called in at 'The Bull'?

DAN: Yes.

DORIS: Very beery, 'The Bull'.

DAN: Yes. Very beery.

DORIS: Oh, Dan! Where did we go wrong?

MAUD GRACECHURCH

CHRISTOPHER FRY

PHILIP: The cow has calved.

JILL: Something decidedly
Sexual is always going on in the cowshed.
Nature never seems to have heard of the
        Pregnancy Advisory service.

PHILIP: Talking of service, is there any coffee?

JILL: There'll be instant in an instant.
        While you're waiting,
Crumble yourself a slice of my seed cake.
Putting seeds into a cake has always
        seemed to me
Appropriately agricultural. So very vernal.
What's this, lettering up the mantelpiece?
You sluthering, post-postponing farm
        manager, you.
Surely you know that the forms on
        deep-littering
Must deeply litter the Ministry doormat
By the twenty-third?

PHILIP: I was unstamped. Only temporarily,
I am glad to report.

HARRISON EVERARD

BEYOND THE PAIL

A recent power crisis prompted the remark that 'there probably isn't a man left in Somerset who could milk a cow by hand'. Interested poets produced comments on this and other country matters.

Inopia Lactis: Rudyard Kipling

There ain't a bloomin' yokel
As'll move 'is bloomin' 'and
To twitch a tit and get some milk
For Blighty's blighted land.

From Somerset to Yorkshire,
From Carlisle to the Strand,
The 'lectric milkin' parlour
Is all they understand.

Now the 'Indoo's not so stupid,
With 'is skinny sacred cow,
For 'e milks 'er with 'is fingers,
And 'e does it even now.

But in England's greener pastures,
Where the cows is much more fat,
The Bolshies 'as electrified,
And that is bleedin' that.

JOHN KING

Since we noo mwore can press the zwitch,
A-cause o' miners' strike,
Ol' Bill an' Tom an' Sam an' sich
Do be vair vlommox'd like.

Ov varmers' plight an' who's to blame,
The mooen cows know nowt,
They vill their milky bags the zame,
But – howe to squeeze zome out?

The dairy's shut, the churns be still,
The milk pails, empty vessels,
Zo I must goo a-down the hill
An' buy a tin o' Nestles'.

An' as I zip my zimple cup,
I'll pray to Wilberforce,
Lest fumblen hands should bugger up
Our whwolesome pinta's source.

STANLEY J. SHARPLESS

Behold it, single in the field,
Yon solitary harvester,
That reaped ten acres by itself
Without the least demur!
Alone it cut and bound the grain
And never showed a hint of strain
While all the jealous farmers round
Were overpowered by the sound.

Will no one tell me how it starts?
Perhaps these mystic numbers stand
For old and discontinued parts
No longer in demand:
Or is it some more humble thing,
Corroded pipe or worn out spring?
Some twisted rod or broken chain
That could be soon put right again?

Whate'er the fault, the makers said
That my old model's not worth mending,
So that is why I'm here, half dead
And o'er this sickle bending.

G. J. S. ROSS

A LOT TO OFFER

Competitors were invited to attempt to sell, in the language of the holiday brochure, any well-known public figure.

Overweight? Puffy-faced? Short of breath? Too much port and pheasant, chicken and cream? Then come to bracing Margaret Thatcher, Queen of the British Hydros, for the slimming cure par excellence! Children with puppy fat especially welcome. Margaret Thatcher gives you the delight of a regimen free from that deadly fattener, milk, and makes austerity a pleasure. Enjoy the experience of walking again – yes, there are buses, but you won't want to use them! – devour sandwich lunches – yes, there are hot, properly cooked meals, but Margaret Thatcher makes them seem unnecessary. Give up your pints and lose your pounds with bright, breezy, compelling Margaret Thatcher!

G. J. BLUNDELL

For the ideal motorists' motorist, come to NABARRO. This external combustion engined, outstandingly scenic, magnificently anticlockwise personage and genuine reproduction English Sir is at the centre of the carpeted industry. The bosky bonnet is artistically landscaped, with well-trimmed radiator muff and neatly sculptured tweed trim. A fleet of splendidly maintained luxury transport vehicles, chauffeur driven or self-drive, is included, with exciting gains on the roundabouts to compensate for losses on the swings to Labour. With guaranteed self-satisfaction, built-in waffle and chucklehead exhaust baffle, this superb example of an obsolescent – some say obsolete – model is, it is confidently believed and hoped, a never to be repeated acquisition, to be nabbed while the going is good.

TOM BREWER

You are probably the sort of person who expects to get real satisfaction from a celebrity. Choosy. Discriminating. The sort of customer we like. And we think you will appreciate the celebrity we've chosen for you this year. In fact we feel that we can ABSOLUTELY GUARANTEE that you will enjoy ravishing Miss Germaine Greer. Her unspoilt natural odours will delight you. Her craggy independence of mind charms, but stops short of disconcerting, and her appealing unconventionality doesn't mean she is unaware what comfort money can buy. This year, let Germaine Greer bend you, just a bit, from your straight and narrow path.

JOHN KING

GIRL ABOUT TOWN

An extract from the diary of a typical 'Cosmo' girl

11th: Terrific party Simon's.

12th: Arrived home 8.30 a.m. The Ageds completely lost cool. Left home 8.30. With luggage. Never darken etc. Simon's pad – nobody in. To office, changed & remade face in loo. Boss livid late arrival . . . Left in dudgeon 9.50: Fab new job Rookstours 11 a.m. Fantastic boss. Giles. Took dictation on his knee. Three times. 4th share birdcage with Fiona, Jen and Penny. Bt roll carpet on way home. Jeremy called. 6-7 laid carpet. 7-7.30 laid Jeremy. On to Tina's. Very artistic. Had bet with Alastair whether Michelangelo's David circumcised. Won. Whether Fiona's Peter is. Won. Whether p. 346 *Kama Sutra* physically possible. Lost.

13th: Fab party St Muke's Hosp. Won 1st prize raffle, free abortion. On to Liz's at Slough. Jeremy spray-painted HEATH PUBLIC ENEMA No 1 across M4. Liz researching article for her paper on sexual responses of the male to fast sports car travel.

WILLIAM HODSON

WHAT'S A SAILORS' PARTY? POMPIDOU

'Who hates trumpets?' 'Géricault'. An excruciating New York game involved inventing questions-and-answers on this model. Further ones were liberally supplied.

What makes an ex-President melancholy? – Mrs Whitehouse.

Say, man, wha's yo' position in de fiel', den? – De Gaulle.

EVELYN WARD

What might one order in a bierkeller? – Einstein.

D. J. JACKSON

Fox-hunting's a jolly good sport? Sez who? – Cézanne.

MAURICE HALL

What do spiders do while awaiting their prey? – Sidney Webb.

Briefly, Captain, how would you define low morale? – Liddell Hart.

JACK BLACK

What sort of noise does an old French war-horse make? – Marshal Ney.

M. YELSAP

W-w-when w-w-will you b-b-be f-f-finished c-c-cutting m-m-my hair? – Sassoon.

Which poet invented preventatives? – Thomas Hood.

NAOMI MARKS

Where do magistrates get their clothes? – A. J. P. Taylor.

What does an Australian doctor say to an English patient when he wants a urine specimen? – Pompidou.

B. D. SYLVESTER

Of what does Pat Nixon live in daily dread? – Henry Kissinger.

And who was that I saw you accosting in Piccadilly last night, Mr Gladstone? – A. Trollope.

What does a badly mangled epigram make? – Oscar Wilde.

MARTIN FAGG

What do the Italians call the East Sussex Orchestra? – Hastings Banda.

HEATHE

How do you greet a Lord Chancellor? – Hailsham.

KEN MACKENZIE

How do you arrive at British Summer Time? – Adenauer.

JAMES DOWELL

How did the Byrd get revenge on the cat? – He Claude Debussy.

SYMIAN HEEK

How do you topple a French Republic? – Poujard.

MARTIN REYNOLDS

What is likely to be unusual about next year's Oxford boat race crew? – Ella Wheeler Wilcox.

H. O. DONAL

Lift a policeman's skirt and what do you find? – Copernicus.

F. A. V. MADDEN

Would you care to sum up in a word your opinion of this dramatist's plays? – Corneille.

What feature of England causes most complaints from American tourists? – Stratford Johns.

J. M. CROOKS

In which tent do the public vote? – General Booth.

C. L. BUNDELA

What's the secret of Italian cooks? – Pasternak.

DAVID MATTHEWS

Where are left-wing actors buried? – Redgraves.

Are you working on your gospel, Matthew? – Omar Khayyam.

MICHAEL GROSVENOR MYER

THERE WAS A CROOKED MAN

**Nursery rhymes inspired by Watergate which would be
current 100 years hence**

Mikes in the ceiling,
Mikes in the floor,
Mikes beneath the sofa,
Mikes behind the door,
Mikes up the chimney,
Mikes beneath the chairs,

Mikes in the passage,
Mikes up the stairs,
Mikes behind the bookcase,
Mikes in the wall –
Tell us what you know, Dick.
I know bugger all.

Dickie was a bugger,
Dickie was a crook,
You'll never bag a bigger bugger
However far you look.

STANLEY J. SHARPLESS

Fiddle diddle dumpling
My son Dick,
Bought two houses,
Both on tick.
From a white house
To the Nick
Ain't too far for
My son Dick.

JAMES SKINNER

Sing a song of Watergate,
A closet full of tapes.
Dick and Dave and Johnnie,
Getting into scrapes.

When the lid was blown off,
The crap it hit the fan.
Wasn't that a can of worms
For poor old Uncle Sam?

JACK BLACK

APPROPRIATE ANAGRAMS

Anagrams of the names of historical figures and in some way appropriate to the characters from which they come

William Shakespeare – I like Mr W. H. as a pal, see?

N. J. BYARD

Helen of Troy – Horny to feel.
Marie Antoinette – Er, I mean *Not* eat it!

TOM BREWER

Oscar Fingal O'Flaherty Wills Wilde – Tell Carson Alfie was wholly frigid.

C. J. FARRELL

Lytton Strachey – That corny style.
Mao Tse-tung – Must not age.

IAIN COLLEY

Norman Mailer – Normal Marine.
Andy Warhol – A Randy Howl.

JACK BLACK

Martin Luther – Learn, I'm truth.

E. MILLER

Samuel Taylor Coleridge – Rage on, ye cold mute sailor.

ROSEMARY NALDEN

Marie Stopes – I see to prams.

LORRAINE DAVIS

Yoko Ono – O.K. O! Oy! No!!

SHAIE SELZER

Neville Chamberlain – Have Berlin call me in.

LEO T. BURKE

Lord George-Brown – Gr-grow old on beer.

DAVID PHILLIPS

Harold Macmillan – Charmin' old llama.

FG

William Shakespeare – A weakish speller, am I?

M. YELSAP

SHE IS COMING, MY OWN, MY SWEET

According to William S. Baring-Gould, Tennyson 'is supposed to have written many fine erotic limericks . . . but all of them were destroyed soon after his death.' Competitors provided examples by Tennyson and other Eminent Victorians

An old poet called Omar cried, 'Now
I've found Paradise truly, and how
   I regret what I said –
   Stuff the verse, wine and bread,
I'll have thou, and have thou, and have thou.'

EDWARD FITZGERALD
(J.E.C.)

A. E. HOUSMAN

A Salopian student of Greek
Had a love of Hellenic physique;
   And many a Lad
   In Ludlow he had
By the dint of his classic technique.

TIM O'DOWDA

A tribute to MATTHEW ARNOLD
in a moment of self-abuse:

A scholar of Oxford, while tipsy,
Began to make love to a gipsy;
   He undressed her, caressed her,
   To the beach he had pressed her,
Then found he'd lost faith in his ipse.

RICHARD SHEPHERD

GENERAL GORDON

Some people think I'm a bit la-di-
Da; others say I'm quite hardy.
   The truth is, in brief:
   I'm seeking relief,
But not at the hands of the Mahdi.

C. VITA-FINZI

*Could there be one from the Most Eminent
Victorian of them all . . . ?*

'Dear Prince Albert of Saxe-Coburg-Gotha,
We desire to receive Our full quota
   Of amorous sport,
   And not be kept short
By one tittle or jot or iota.'

JAMES SKINNER

Her limp lover Maud couldn't pardon.
He was no use at all in the garden
   But drooped like the rose
   When the sap in it goes.
'Ere, Enoch!' she cried, 'Enoch, 'arden!'

KIT WRIGHT

The Last Ride Together

'Is it thou?' 'Ay,' cried Fra Lippo Lippi,
'Zooks, lass, 'tis confoundedly nippy.
   But slip out of your gown
   And I'll give you a crown
Or two more; but we'd best make it slippy.'

So they up and went at it like knives.
Or they humped (shall I say?) 'sthough
                            their lives
   Were dependent on what
   They performed; and they got
To the climax in just twenty drives

Of the loins. She sighed, *'Flower of the vine,*
My God! You are perfectly mine;
   'Tis enough. Keep your gold.
   But my love, I grow cold.
Where's 'e gone? Where's my gown?
                 Br-r-r you swine!'

JEDEDIAH BARROW

The rose gives a tremulous glance
And sighs, 'He is lost in a trance!'
   'Let us wait,' cries the pink,
   'He is coming, I think!'
But the passion-flower weeps.
               'Not a chance!'

ANNE NORRIS

'I would doubt,' said the Bishop of Balham,
'If Tennyson ever had Hallam.
   Such things are best hid:
   Still let's hope that he did –
De mortuis nil nisi malum.'

TERENCE RATTIGAN

Patriotic Address From the Banks of the Silver Tay

O! Great Queen! Whom I idolise!
'Twould be a most pleasant Surprise,
   And one to remember,
   Could I place my Member
Between thy Mighty and Sovereign Thighs.

W. S. McGONAGALL (Poet & Tragedian)
(JEFFREY LITTMAN)

UNTAKEUPABLE

The most off-putting book-blurbs possible

Good Friday. A storm off the Clare coast. A wreck! A lone survivor swims ashore, gripping between his teeth a cloth bundle. He drowns in the shallows. Villagers drag him ashore. Ripping open his precious bundle, they discover a small wet puppy – alive!

The pup's winning presence transforms the moribund little community. He is christened in church on Easter Sunday, and adopted by the parish.

In a surge of wild humour and passionate poetry Miss O'Raihilli recounts the ramifications of Fidelis's influence. He effects the conversion of curmudgeonly old atheist, Martin, rescuing him after a fall when collecting samphire; protects the virtue of fey, half-witted Dympna, the village sweetheart, snapping at the heels of a too-ardent Tommy Big-Eyes; reunites the feuding O'Farrells; discovers Mad Bridie's corpse; brings new joy to Widow M'Guire; and many other adventures.

His mysterious death, his funeral and wake, and the subsequent miracle are touchingly rendered.

ANNE B. RODGERS

You don't *have* to be a Fellow of All Souls to read this book – but it helps. For here, at last, is the ultimate in experimental novels, the logical and final successor of the book whose chapters could be arranged in any order. In *Anag.* by H. J. S. Nobson the *words*, even the letters, can and indeed must be re-arranged before the novel's true subtlety and complexity can be revealed. From the first brilliantly evocative phrase 'Can I open me out?' – perceptive readers will instantly unravel the words 'Once upon a time' – through 900 pages of incredible depth and difficulty *Anag.* makes all other novels look absurdly facile and superficial. The supreme tribute to H. J. S. Nobson's work is surely that critics have been inspired to comment in his own style (short though their efforts fall of the Master's touch): Margaret Drabble said of *Anag.* 'Great Ramble, Bard', Kingsley Amis said 'Yes, liking a MS', while A. Waugh said 'Awa', Ugh!' (This blurb can of course be re-interpreted like all Nobson's writings.)

J. M. CROOKS

Mungo, a breeder of poisonous spiders, is in love with one or other of the identical twins Philomena and Amaryllis, neither of whom, however, is able to reciprocate his passion as they are both besotted with Karlheinz, a blind abortionist from Dusseldorf. Unfortunately, Karlheinz's own affections are bestowed on the enigmatic Sylvia, who never actually appears in the book but whose presence is strongly felt as the focal point around which the other characters endlessly revolve.

But *An Unrequited Love* is more than a brilliant entertainment, posing as it does some of the fundamental moral dilemmas of our time. How well can we ever really know ourselves? Does love have a strange ambivalent power for both good and evil? Who is Sylvia? The surprising answers to these and many other questions make Iris Murdoch's 24th novel the most riveting literary event since Wittgenstein's *Tractatus Logicophilosophicus*.

BRIAN ALLGAR

ABOVE THE BELT

Printable limericks of good taste, elegance, wit and humour were requested, modelled, more or less, on the following:

**There were once two young people of taste
Who were beautiful down to the waist.
So they limited love
To the regions above
And thus remained perfectly chaste.**

A couple from old Aberystwyth
United the organs they kissed with,
   They enjoyed this sweet sharing
   But did nothing more daring
And she said 'You're a right one to tryst with'.

                    STUART WOODS

An artist who haunted Montmartre
Made improper suggestions to Sartre,
   But Sartre with a blow
   At his hanging *huis clos*
Cut his two existentials apartre.

                SIR JOHN WALLER BT

Undressing a maiden called Sue,
Her seducer exclaimed 'If it's true
   That a nipple a day
   Keeps the doctor away,
Think how healthy you must be with two!'

                  BRIAN ALLGAR

A Hi-Fi fanatic called Peter
Proudly showed his equipment to Rita,
   But he felt quite forlorn
   When his woofer lacked horn
And he seemed to have lost his left tweeter.

               MARGARET ROGERS

A popular girl is Miss Cholmondeley,
She's youthful, attractive and colmondeley,
   And never objects
   To suggestions of sex
But simply cooperates dolmondeley,

                SALLY McKINLEY

'How much,' sighed the handsome Narcissus,
'A man of my character misses.
   It's clear on reflection
   I've got an erection,
But all I can do is blow kisses.'

             STEPHEN SYLVESTER

Few people could hope to compare
With the two who made love on the stair.
  When the bannister broke
  They thought it a joke
And carried on with panache in mid air.

J. ENDERSBY

Widow (conscious that time's on the wing),
Fortyish, but still game for a fling,
  Seeks fun-loving male,
  Mature, but not stale,
With a view to the usual thing.

STANLEY J. SHARPLESS

Wanting children, a couple once sat
For a course on how they were begat.
  When the doctor expounded
  They stood up dumbfounded
And said they could never do *that*.

G. W. HANNEY

A lad of the brainier kind
Had erogenous zones in the mind.
  He loved the sensations
  Of solving equations.
(Of course, in the end, he went blind.)

HYMIE SNEAK

A Texan Rhodes Scholar named Fred
Was a witty companion in bed.
  With priapic zest
  He would toss off each jest:
'I'm standing for congress,' he said.

LYNDON T. MOLE

There once was a maid of Bahari
Who was chased on a night that was starry.
  She was chaste, so she raced,
  Tore her gown in her haste
And cried, 'Really I *must* go – sew sari.'

R. P. M. LEHMANN

TWO HORNS IN HARMONY

The sensational novel *Philharmonic* concerned the lives and loves of the members of an orchestra. Competitors provided extracts from novels dealing with the private lives of other unlikely professional groups.

Tube

There were no passengers on the down train. Carlos seized her by the arm, his brown fingers feeling through the roughness of her uniform for the warmth that was quivering beneath. They ran into the automatic lift just as the doors began to close. The half-naked girls on the walls made him feel foolishly self-conscious; but Nora was already dragging him down, sly lips whispering 'Hurry along now, please'. His frantic breath, he suddenly saw, blew a ticket along the floor like a leaf in a tropical storm; his heart beat loud, like wheels on unwelded track. Even Nora could hear it, for she was cocking her head in a way that reminded him of that overpowering moment when he had first . . . what was she saying? 'It's Ted. I can hear him. He's running up the emergency stairs. What are we going to do?'

C. VITA-FINZI

Habit!

'Pissed again, Sister Theresa!'
There was envy rather than anger in the Mother Superior's voice.
'Sorry, Reverend' – hic – 'Mother. They had this party at St Swithin's.'
'Right old rave, was it?' The Mother Superior's eyes gleamed with curiosity over the joint she was rolling. Her tongue snaked lasciviously along its length.
'Wild! You know what those monks are like – Benedictine flowed like holy water.'
Sister Theresa leaned back yawning, her full breasts thrusting against the thick cloth of her habit.
'Christ, I'm bushed! Brother Anthony wouldn't let me out of his cell – talk about the Passion of Our Lord!'
The Mother Superior's hand slid gently along Theresa's thigh.
'You're wasting your time with him, dear. What do men know about love?'
'Not much,' Theresa smiled ruefully, 'but I try to be catholic. Well, I suppose I'd better go and light a candle.'
'Oh, talking of candles' said the Mother Superior . . .

NAOMI MARKS

School

'I think the work you're doing with the Fourth Year in Mathematics is first-class, Miss Tushington. The way you've fired the interest of those youngsters in Set Theory is the most exciting thing I've seen since I became headmaster.'

'That's sweet of you. But in Sets we are giving them a new language, and after all language is not only the stuff of communication, it is the stuff of thought.'

'True. It could be the most important development since Western man abandoned Roman numerals for Arabic. I wish I knew more about it'.

'There's a residential course at Brighton in the holidays. I thought I might go. Look, Headmaster, why don't you come too?'

'What? Just the two of us, you mean?'

'Why not?'

'Well, I'm not sure that it would be quite professional. After all, I shouldn't be in bed with you now, really.'

J. D. CRISPIN

Bank!

From her desk she could see the counter space where Bernard, helped by the messenger, was unloading heavy canvas bags from the trolley to stow them beneath his till. Her eyes left the Impersonal Debits to focus on the small muscular buttocks outlined by the tightly-stretched dark suiting with its almost indiscernible pin stripe. The exertion had caused his glasses to mist over and as he took them off to polish them she noticed again the steely glint in his dark blue eyes. She pictured the heading of a joint account: Bernard Newby Smith, Esq. and Mrs Daphne Smith.

Later, in a quiet corner where she was filing cancelled cheques, he sought her out. She heard his fast breathing behind her as his hands slipped under her cardigan.

'Not now, Bernard, not now,' she whispered. 'But soon, when the Half Yearly Balance is quite over . . .'

SALLY McKINLEY

FOUL FARE

Competitors devised disgusting dishes which combined pleasant ingredients in a horrible manner – mashed pea ice cream, semolina with parsnips, etc.

Shrimp and Raspberry Cocktail

Line glasses with fresh young turnip-tops. Mix chopped shrimps and raspberries together with cheese sauce, and sprinkle with chicory.

Cream of Oyster Soup

Poach oysters ($\frac{1}{2}$ dozen per person) in bacon stock. Drain. With the liquid make a thin oatmeal porridge. Add oysters and one uncooked banana per person. Put all through liquidiser and serve with tomato sauce.

Mandarin Kidneys

Skin and core sheep's kidneys – 2 or 3 per person. Stuff with mandarin segments from tinned mandarins. Reserve juice. Grill kidneys lightly and place in fireproof dish. Heat together fruit juice and equal quantity single cream. Pour over kidneys. Cover completely with marshmallows and place under grill until a crust forms. Serve with French fried potatoes.

Erebus Pudding

Blancmange with kipper sippets deep-fried in batter. Serve cold with chocolate sauce.

DROMORE

Soupe au pied de Cochon

Pack a pig's trotter with raisins and candied peel in an airtight container. Remove after three days and boil in two pints of milk until skin forms. Remove skin. Continue boiling and skimming until milk is used up. Chill skin and serve as cold coup in liquidised cucumber and bone marrow.

Huitres au Chocolat

Remove oysters from shells and roll in chocolate vermicelli and hundreds and thousands. Serve on slices of beetroot in aspic cubes.

Poulet Maritime

Roast chicken stuffed with pilchards and chicory.

Tapioca Duchesse

Prepare tapioca in the classic way, adding two teaspoonfuls of gelatine to every cup of milk. Set in individual moulds and serve with sponge fingers and crème de menthe butter.

JAMES LOADER

CHINATOWN

Poems in the classical Chinese manner about any aspect
of contemporary London life

Afternoon at the Club

The many-hued flower stands boldly before us;
She is stripping her petals one by one.
Twisting and swaying in the breeze of our
                                                        yearning,
She will soon be only a pliant stem.
As every petal is plucked and flung,
The instruments bray their shrill delight.
Is it because they are thinking of autumn,
That all who gaze should look so sad?

                                    ANDREW McEVOY

When I was a girl I sat with the old men.
Or watching my cherry blossom
I would play with your ts'ing*.
When the birds flew westward
I came to the Province of So Ho
Where no cherry is to be found.
But the old men turned up.
They rose like carp to the feeding hand.
Now after too many months I sit alone.
I mark the days on my calendar.
When you read these words
Clasp your ts'ing and come.

                    *An instrument, similar to a d'ong
                                    but smaller. (trans.)

                                    JEDEDIAH BARROW

The pleasure is not in the waiting

Waiting for a bus at London Bridge
I see afar the winter birds poised
against the heavy sky.
Old newspapers dance round my feet.
You ask me why I stand here
When I could have caught a train.
While I wait I hope,
Besides, the trains are cancelled.
The city sky-line is altering now
from rounded domes and fluted pillars
To square tall blocks of a thousand eyes.
It is too cold to wait any longer.

                        LIAM MAGUIRE

To a Gas Fitter, Conversion Unit No. 9

Since you, sir, went away,
The light of my cooker has gone out.
Only my longing burns like the sea flame;
Will you ever come back?

                        ROSEMARY DINNAGE

1974

TALK WITH KINGS

Kenneth Harris's conversations with Prince Charles were prominently serialised in two parts in *The Observer.* **Similar interviews were conducted with famous figures of the past.**

Alfred

You're virtually in hiding here on Athelney, sir. How do you pass your time?

One sings a bit, you know. Helps with the cooking and plans for the future. And reads.

What sort of things?

The Moderns, mostly. Bede and so on. Though I've got Gregory's *Regula Pastoralis* at the moment. One feels one might like to have a crack at a translation some time.

Do you see any likelihood of your getting your kingdom back?

One likes to think so. We have some first-class chaps working on it and one is always optimistic.

If you ever rule Wessex again what reforms would you like to see?

Ultimately, I think, we shall have to have chaps in ships sailing up and down the coast to keep the Scandinavian types away. One might call it the navy. Don't suppose it will come in my day.

GEORGE VAN SCHAICK

Henry V

. . . at Harfleur?

Well, I suppose I can let the secret out now. It was actually my
PRO who made the speech, dressed in some of my old kit, with the
visor down. He never revealed this, for the simple reason that he got a
bucket of hot lead over him shortly after, poor chap. He wrote the thing
as well, of course overdid it a bit I thought, but the media took it,
and they say it even got into a play. I was still abed, actually, because
we'd had quite a beat-up in the mess the night before. When I put
my head out in the morning and heard all the alarums and things, I
knew my nerve-endings wouldn't stand it, so I went back. Anyway my
2 i/c knew the form. I might just have got in the way. And we won,
didn't we? That was the object of the exercise.

W. S. BROWNLIE

Elizabeth I

Would you say your personal reputation for virginity is an advantage or
a disadvantage?

Both, in a way. I'm sorry if that sounds unhelpful, but it's really
depended upon whoever one happened to be dealing with at the time.
How they've reacted to it.

Did it begin by being a sort of gimmick?

No, though it is a bit unusual, I suppose, for someone in my position.
I believe I'm the first to have had it as my particular 'thing'. Richard
was Lion-hearted, and Ethelred had his Unreadiness, and my father was
bluff, amongst other things. I suppose most people in my position have
been virginal sometimes. I've just done it longer.

How do you get your exercise then?

Well, I play a bit for Essex sometimes, and I turn out for Leicester
when I can. Being royal, I'm keen on sport, of course.

M. K. CHEESEMAN

HIDING BEHIND THE BOTTLE

Competitors speculated on what would have happened had the heroes and heroines of literature drunk Dr Jekyll's draught.

'Jeeves,' I called, 'Rally round the young master with a stiff B and S and get the old brain-cells whizzing. Gussie's in trouble again.' He entered with a lurching walk and the sort of face that would have dragged an admiring gasp from a passing gorilla. 'Jeeves,' I cried, 'This is no time for amateur theatricals. You look like that rummy bloke in the play with the low thingummy.' 'I fancy, sir, you mean the monster Caliban, whose forehead, the Bard assures us, was villainous low. However my appearance is not due to any Thespian activity, but to indulgence in a tonic beverage called Buck-U-Uppo left by a Mr Mulliner. Mr Fink-Nottle also called, wearing a tie whose design caused me considerable pain.' 'Live and let live, Jeeves. I trust you were not churlish with him?' 'No, sir. I fear I strangled him with it.'

CLIVE JACQUES

'Wharton!' boomed Mr Quelch. 'Wretched boy! You have been smoking!' 'No, sir', Harry Wharton lied. 'It was those chaps who left as you came through the dorm, Cherry and Bull.' Quivering in his hiding place, Bunter gasped. Harry Wharton was a sneak! 'I had thought,' observed Mr Quelch acidly, 'that I might have had to give you six of the best before you revealed the names of your friends. At least.' 'I didn't want to have to blub, sir. Besides, why should I suffer for those bounders?' 'See me in my study after Prep.,' said Mr Quelch, and departed. 'Now, Bunter,' said Harry Wharton, dragging the Owl of the Remove from behind the curtain, 'and take your bags down.' 'Ow! Urrrgh. Yaroo. You rotten beast!' 'As Coker said down at the pub today, there's a lot of things I've been missing at Greyfriars, up till now.'

ROBIN CHASE

They had settled in armchairs at each side of a cheerful fire, the Rat
trying to find a rhyme for something or other and the Mole toasting
muffins for tea. Suddenly, the half finished verses slipping from
his knee, the Rat reached to the corner cupboard and took
a deep draught from a bottle which the Mole had not seen before.
'Mole, old chap,' he said, 'have you ever wondered why I
invited you, a total stranger, to live here rent-free, using my
boat, meeting my friends?' His eyes had a sinister glint,
his snout seemed unexpectedly longer, his teeth more pointed.
'I know Ratty, that you are the kindest . . .'
Mole realised for the first time how much bigger
Water Rats were than himself. 'Did I tell you
before,' snarled Ratty, 'how much I've always
fancied a moleskin smoking jacket?'

GEORGE VAN SCHAICK

133

HELLO YOUNG LOVERS

Love scenes for characters from children's books

'To the woods!' said William.

'What for?' said Violet Elizabeth. 'Are you going to play with me?'

'We're going to rape you,' said William. 'Aren't we, Ginger?'

'Course,' said Ginger, dutifully.

'What's wape?' lisped Violet Elizabeth. Clearly, William had aroused her interest.

William hesitated. 'Well – er,' he said. 'Everyone knows what rape is, don't they, Ginger?'

'Course,' replied Ginger. 'Everyone knows that.'

He, William, wished he had been able to see what Robert and his latest girl-friend had actually been *doing* when he, William, watched them through the window of his, Robert's, car, parked in the drive the previous evening.

But Violet Elizabeth was having misgivings. 'I'll thcream and thcream till I'm thick,' she said. 'I *can*,' she added.

'How loud can you scream?' asked William.

Violet Elizabeth screamed, not very loudly.

'To the woods!' said William. 'C'mon, Ginger!'

*   *   *   *

'Crumbs!' said William. 'She *has* been "thick".'

TOM LAWRENCE

'Off with her clothes!' roared the Queen.

'How very strange!' exclaimed Alice.

'Who is that impertinent young girl?' demanded the Queen, 'and why is she wearing so many clothes?'

'Chimneys are her thing,' leered the white rabbit, 'she likes putting her foot up them.'

'*Chacun à son flue*,' remarked the Queen, and began to do things with a hedgehog which Alice did not altogether like.

'What curious people!' Alice could not restrain herself from saying out loud. The king, who had been looking at Alice with vigorous interest since the white rabbit's remark, murmured to her: 'I am a curious fellow. And while we're on the subject, how do you like the look of those soldiers over there?' Alice saw a soldier, doubled-up, and moving his head against the midriff of another soldier.

'The croquet hoops have become tangled up!' said the king, and absently began to play croquet with himself . . .

J. Y. WATSON

'Why are you and Peggy called the Amazons, Nancy?'

'Well, it certainly isn't because we've cut one breast off!' Nancy laughed merrily and continued to whittle her jibstay. 'Oh, I know *that*', John said impatiently. 'Peggy showed me when you were caulking Captain Flint's bottom. She's the one who ought to be called Titty.'

'If it comes to that, why are you called the Swallows?' 'That was Susan's idea,' John admitted. 'It was after she saw some film that really impressed her – *Deep Boat* I think it was called.'

'Shiver my timbers! You're still a bit of a landlubber aren't you?' Nancy whacked John playfully with her jibstay. 'Look, let's pop into your tent and I'll show you what Susan really meant . . .'

A scream rent the air. 'But, Nancy,' John stammered. 'You are . . . you are . . . a *boy*!' 'Of course I am. Why do you think I'm called Nancy, duckie?'

J. M. CROOKS

SPACIOUS PREMISES

An estate agent's prospectus for the planet earth as it stands at present

Four-cornered estate of well-rounded appearance in spacious surroundings, close to galactic centre and with unobscured views of tastefully star-studded universe. Two-sevenths occupied, remainder with vacant possession. Some damp. Full set of latitudes and meridians; N and S poles (planning permission for more if required). Sitting tenants number approx. 3,500,000,000, in tied accommodation. Estate at present worked on the basis of a reliable 24-hour turnover and annual orbit. Many fine early natural features (Cambrian, Jurassic, etc.) with spectacular additions and improvements (Egyptian, Roman, Victorian, etc., and Modern): human contributions full of atmosphere. Atmosphere, full of human contributions. Mature eco-system, free inexhaustible solar energy supply with very popular underground storage feature. Inhabited continents on solid foundations with built-in 'drift', each possessing well-contrasted social, political, and religious practices offering much scope for creative tension.

GUDRUN FIRMANI

FOR SALE: Charming old world, extensively modernised throughout, situated among quiet neighbours in desirable Milky Way. Many novel fixtures added to original structure. Adjacent satellite convenient for disposal of technological waste. Large tracts of planet already completely cleared of vegetation, and current defoliation programme should soon remove the rest. Abundant water supply, some plain, but most ready salted. Unique solar heating system provides automatic variable temperature control. Vacant possession soon, pending imminently expected demise of present tenants. Suit retired little green men. Regret no coloureds. Apply Dominus, Filius, and S. Sanctus, Estate Agents.

R. F. LEACH

BE YOUR AGE

**Cautionary verses from a modern *Struwwelpeter* and addressed
not to children but to parents**

Louise declared, with gestures wild,
She'd ne'er breast-feed her infant child!
'The thought,' she cried, 'that my fine bust
Might sag, quite fills me with disgust.'
'Beware!' they said, 'vain pride so dire
Will rouse the Great Earthmother's ire:
She'll pounce on those who bottle-feed,
De-busting them with horrid speed!'
Too true! As Lou the feed prepared,
The Great Earthmother at her glared,
And seizing her despite her tears,
Chomped off those much-prized hemispheres!

F. GALWAY

Myfanwy Cripps, though in her teens,
Was still enjoined to 'eat her greens'.
(Her mother's muddled mental stock
Was not just old but ante-Spock!)
To end the daily incubus
Of this ignoble mealtime fuss,
She gassed her parents; then she sowed 'em
With spinach seed and mulched and hoed 'em;
Then watched them sprouting with aplomb,
Sold all the crop and made a bomb.
And now she waits expectantly
To see them raise some broccoli.

TIM O'DOWDA

BROADENING THE MIND

**Travel articles written with the sort of breezy vulgarity
that sometimes occurs in them**

In the main square of Chutsk where one of Attila's armies once ravished 12,000 virgins in a single afternoon (such an unsuitable time!), you can buy scrumptious locally-fired cooking pots that out-Habitat Habitat; you will be hard put to it to find half a dozen such girls nowadays (should that be your quest). The cathedral steps are sheer *Battleship Potemkin*, though not as slippery. John (*Stones of Venice*) Ruskin hated the façade of this cathedral, which is dedicated to St Oswain, who was immolated on a seed harrow (very painful, I would have thought!). Inside, soak yourself in the Bezzolini font where D. H. (*Sons and Lovers*) Lawrence is said to have washed his feet, though Katherine (*The Garden Party*) Mansfield said it was too small. The faces of the painted and gilded supporting cherubs (the colours are worthy of Heals!) reminded me of The (*Penny Lane*) Beatles!

HARRISON EVERARD

We left Valladolid with memories of beggars in hunchback alleys, of rough purple wine, and of a meal of roast kid, beans and cool green figs eaten at an inn outside the town where mule train drivers, dusty farmboys and ancient women muffled in rusty black dipped hunks of bread into a communal stew. On the road south, which cuts through vast, brazen wheatfields, straight as Valentino's parting, the sun beat down on the Jensen until it felt like a white-hot ingot beaten on an anvil and only its air-conditioning saved us.

We entered Segovia by the Puerto de Santiago, as Cervantes must often have done, and Noël was impressed by the aqueduct in a curious child-like way as if he had been a tourist. In the back streets naked children fled into decrepit houses, for all the world like pheasants running for cover on Freddie's Wiltshire acres at home.

GEORGE VAN SCHAICK

Fun-loving people are choosing Iceland this year. Few things are more satisfying than discussing your favourite saga over a lager in Skjöldölfsstadhir while a friendly neighbourhood geyser spouts boiling water and steam high into the air (you can understand why the old Icelandic bards were called 'skalds'). I popped into the Althing, the oldest parliament in the world (Althing – 'old thing' – see how easy Icelandic is?) and found I was able to follow a debate on the 50-mile limit almost blow by blow. It was all pure Magnus Magnusson. Then I nipped over to Hjardharholt to visit the grave of Isleifr Gissurarson whose work I've admired since a child. Back then for a fish supper at Isafjördhur with Ari Thorgilsson whose latest movie (or cod-piece as he deprecatingly calls it) is currently wowing them in the aisles in the Reykjavik Odeon.

STANLEY J. SHARPLESS

NONE BUT

Lonely-hearts advertisements from well-known persons, living or dead

Clairaudient, clairvoyant but anglophobic French virgin; interests: agriculture, martial arts, transvestism, theology, kingship and nationalism, would like to meet sincere and strong Catholic celibates to practise all-in wrestling and other physical pursuits.

RUSSELL LUCAS

Gent, early sixties, after years of affliction, seeks youthful companion (preferably female) aristocratic but not stuffy, command of French and total respect for discipline, for new happiness and mutual exploration in cheerful rural asylum. Apply M. de S.

GEORGE MOOR

Jewish hippie, late twenties; interested mysticism, politics, public speaking; hobbies conjuring, water-skiing; seeks applicants for all-male mobile commune; object peaceful revolution; no objection to straights.

DAN ROSENBERG

Austrian painter (ex-soldier, two good war records) interested in politics. Tolerant type, non-smoker, vegetarian, teetotaller, seeks blonde lady. No Jews, Catholics, Communists, Marxists, Liberals, Conservatives, need apply.

PETER J. DONOGHUE

Occasionally retiring but incisive Victorian gent seeks female companionship in East End. Has unaccountably difficult problems forming stable relationships with opposite sex, but rarely fails to leave lasting impression. Rendezvous in strictest confidence.

B. SAMUEL

Bachelor, mathematician, children's writer, amateur photographer, wishes meet widow with daughter under 12. View quiet picnics on river and some modelling by 'little lady'. Mother's age, appearance immaterial, but daughter should have long, shiny hair, appealing eyes and slim figure.

DAN HAZLEWOOD

PILGRIMS' PROGRESS

Extracts from any modern Canterbury Tale

Portrait of the Pornographer

Ther was a KNIGHT, a worthy for the chaffre.
He lovede gold, and was a Pornografre.
To sellen likerous bokis was his wone,
For he was Daun Boccacces owene sone.
Bretful his mal was, ful of lewed news
And images of swivings and of screws.
To Stokholme hadde he been on pilgrimage,
And comen was to delen us outrage –
Of *flagellatio* and swich hethnesse,
De coitu and other cursedness,
As in our dayes is nat worth a torde.
He balled was, and highte
                          LORD LONGENFORDE

                    G. W. JONES

The Hicche-Hykeres Tale

This yonge fresshe wenche, wel loking
                          honey-swete,
Hir thumbe up-haf and gan a lifte entrete,
Wherat eftsone oon sely wight dide stoppe
And curteislie, I-wis, bade hir in hoppe.
Quod he, Gode morwe, whider wendestow?
Thanne quod this murie jade, til
                          Marlborrowe
Thereto he syde that she moghte with hym
                          steye
Til Gildforde, wher his destinacioun leye,
Bur whan hem neghen dide to Gildforde toun
She til hir verray queynte up – drow hir goun,
And swoor to crye out Ravyne! and Harrow!
So mote he bere hir ful to Marlborrowe.

          W. F. N. WATSON

The Probatioun Officeres Tale

The lede guiterriste was a craftie ladde,
Wel koude he luren chickes to his padde
To dyg the sownes of Clapton or The Stones
And share a joynte and turn on for the nones,
Till met he wyth a drogge squadde
                          maiden fayre
Who yaf him think she was a Frenssche
                          au pair,
That whan at last he caused hir sens to feynte
And subtilly to frote hir at the queynte,
And whyspere sucred words, and strook
                          her sore,
'Lay on!' she cried, 'my rammysh prikasour!'
For she was nothing loth to amorous sport
So be she got hir Pusheres into court.

          GERARD BENSON

NOW WE ARE SEVEN

**Introductions about various adult activities and
aimed at the seven-year-old child**

I expect mummy's read you the story of how Pooh and Piglet hunted
the woozle. If you were very clever you'd have guessed before she got to
the end that they were chasing their own footprints. That's just what
happens in politics. There's one party like Pooh, who was rather slow
on the uptake and self-satisfied, and another one like Piglet who, although
he had rather more sense, felt such a puny little chap by comparison
that, try as he might, he couldn't help thinking Pooh rather a grand
fellow. But unlike Pooh and Piglet, the two parties we're talking about
don't recognise that most of the time they're walking hand in hand in
the same direction and round the same thicket. It's not that either of
them is frightened of the other's footprints – it's just that it sometimes
frightens them when they see their footprints so close together.

JONATHAN SLEIGH

Politics is a game of skill and chance in which you score points for making other players look silly. British champions meet in the Houses of Parliament, a building in London that looks like a church but is really a club. The two main teams are Labour (red) and Conservative (blue). The leader of whichever team is voted winner after five years is called Prime Minister. He can change the rules, but must let the Queen know the score every week. The members who are paid to play (MPs) use one end of the club, and those who do it for fun (the Lords) use the other. Although the Lords are mostly old, they dress up like Prince Charming when the Queen comes to open the first match of the season. Grown-ups write to MPs instead of to Father Christmas. Sometimes they get what they ask for.

MARGARET ROGERS

Foreign travel is very educational. The first thing you learn is that foreign countries have just as much rain as Britain does. The second is that foreigners don't think it's funny when you tell them so. They are often ignorant. If you learnt French at school you soon find that French people don't understand their own language. Most foreigners seem to work in hotels and cafés, and speak some English, but make comical mistakes. They drive on the wrong side of the road just because their cars have the steering wheel on the left. In Italy they don't have proper food, only spaghetti and pizzas, and of course no foreigners can make a real cup of tea. They drink what they call coffee, but instead of being in tins, they grind up sort of nuts to make it, in tiny cups like a doll's tea-set.

ADAM KHAN

MELLOW FRUITFULNESSES

Sonnets on 'Autumn'

Belfast: Autumn 1974

Already winter's hand is on the town;
Old men are lighting bonfires in the park.
Evenings are chilly, mornings cold and dark;
October's turned the leaves from green to
        brown,
And soon November's gales will bring them
        down.
And in my autumn thoughts there's not a
        spark
Of comfort: all seems desolate and stark
And grimmer far than old December's frown.

Winter was once a time when you and I
Could sit and drink in warm and friendly bars,
And damn the tax collector and the State.
But now we're living in a world of hate,
Where sinister young men in stolen cars
Will come with bombs and some of us will die.

ROBERT BAIRD

Fall

Thy leaves, O Autumn, fall now one by one;
The standing corn falls, into combines fed;
The pheasant from the copse falls to the gun,
Or rain falls, keeping harvesters abed.
Thy temp'rature falls each succeeding day,
Seed falls in furrows from the tractor'd drill,
Fruit falls when at thy breath the
                                    branches sway,
Milk falls in milker, by Amynta's skill.
And as we see these declinations all
When they befall in season at thy hest,
Just so for one more super-special fall
Thou heard'st my plea, and granting my
                                        request
Bade fall for me that which all rapture means:
At nightfall, in the barn, Amynta's jeans.

TOM BREWER

Autumn, Holloway Road

On Highbury Fields damp moulting plane
                                    trees loom
Silent and grim under a tarnished sky;
A shabby salesman in an old school tie
Scurries towards a chilly furnished room.
Grotesquely lolls outside the *Horse and Groom*
Like some symbolic drunk a soggy guy,
While bright-faced children pester passers-by
For pennies in the rainy evening's gloom.
A woman burdened with chrysanthemums
Laughs with her lover, face tilts to his grin;
The steamed-up windows of the Take-Away
Daub yellow on the pavement's slimy grey;
A muttering tramp rifles a garbage bin,
And grimy pigeons squabble over crumbs.

JEDEDIAH BARROW

OUR FAIRLY MUTUAL FRIEND

Extracts from the Dickensian novel, *Edward Heath*

It had long been a moot point among Mr Heath's multifarious acquaintance whether he worked his shoulders or whether they worked him. So unsynchronised were their shakings, so unrelated their convulsions to any true matter of mirth, that it began to be whispered that he carried captive beneath his coat another being – another, earlier version of himself perchance – who, long since battened down beneath the hatches of his ambition, now mostly slumbered – but who occasionally awoke and fought desperately to crack through and escape from the cold carapace of calculation in which he found himself confined. The strain of keeping this hapless prisoner pent within him was thought to have cost Mr Heath dear and to be reflected in his bodily habit. Those shoulders rose and fell; the whole body heaved; the eyes shone remorselessly; and the mouth broadened and beamed. But was it goodwill truly that was radiated? Was the rictus indeed one of laughter – or was it that of a covert and consuming rage?

COLIN KIMBERLEY

'I will never desert Mr Heath,' declared Mrs Thatcher, with vehemence. 'He is leader of my party and captain of my ship.' 'I told them the truth,' repeated Heath. 'Income twenty pounds, expenditure nineteen pounds ninety seven and a half pence . . .' 'Yes, yes,' interposed Whitelaw soothingly, 'one knows.' Hailsham expatiated on Heath's capacities, with frequent references to Charles I, which Heath found not altogether reassuring. 'I have always proclaimed Hailsham's sagacity,' he confided to Whitelaw, 'but I sometimes wonder if he is not, as the world says, "bonkers!" ' 'From my umble position,' insinuated Du Cann, writhing from the waist up, 'I will always support the leader, though I am too umble ever to share his counsel.' 'But one asks,' urged Whitelaw, singularly, 'whether his present position affords sufficient scope for Mr Heath's remarkable talents. Perhaps a different arena . . .?' Heath paled. 'Not Australia?' 'One was thinking of the Lords.'

R. F. LEACH

'My dear Willie,' said Mr Heath with unaccustomed fervour, 'I have no desire to resign, though I am well aware that you and other loyal spirits may, after a protracted inner struggle, fall victims to political pressures of a complicated nature. I regret it, but I can bear it.' 'Edward!' exclaimed Mr Whitelaw, in tears, 'Have I deserved this? I, who have never deserted you; who will *never* desert you, Edward!' 'My dear friend and colleague,' said Mr Heath, much affected, 'you will forgive the momentary laceration of a wounded spirit, made sensitive by the scarcely veiled hints and promptings of Mr du Cann's committee, and will pity, not condemn, my anxiety.' Mr Heath then embraced Mr Whitelaw, but I could hardly fail to notice that Mr Whitelaw's returning pat on his shoulder was less a gesture of assurance than a surreptitious seeking after a suitable spot to place the knife.

NAOMI MARKS

SECOND BESTS

Breathes there a man with soul so dead
Who was not, in the Thirties, Red?
Competitors provided further unlikely second lines to well-known firsts

That's my last Duchess painted on the wall,
Ignore those artist's boobs! She had none at all.

                    D. G. BULL

Break off, break off this last lamenting kiss,
I'm absolutely dying for a piss.

                    BRENDAN GORSE

And did those feet in ancient time
Ache as much as yours and mine?

                    MARTIN SHERWOOD

I stood in Venice, on the Bridge of Sighs;
Above my feet I felt the waters rise.

                    ROBERT GITTINGS

Stands the church clock at ten to three?
Does no one wind the thing but me?

                    PETER VEALE

Let us now praise famous men
And give a mensh. to Tony Benn.

                    P. W. R. FOOT

Bliss was it in that dawn to be alive,
Struggling to catch the 7.45.

                    ROY DEAN

A thing of beauty is a joy forever
And sold, evades all Gains Tax if you're clever.

Shall I compare thee to a summer's day?
You fit the bill – cold, dimmish, wet and grey.

                    MARTIN FAGG

I must go down to the sea again, to
    the lonely sea and the sky,
For if I stop in Downing Street,
    they'll lynch me by-and-by.

                    ANDREW McEVOY

The grave's a fine and private place,
But ashes take up far less space.

                    W. J. WEBSTER

I PREFER BEN HIM

The *Daily Mirror* film guide is apt to provide a breathless plot-summary ending in a pun. Various classics were so treated.

The Sheik: Bored little rich girl abducted by he-Bedouin Valentino to silken-tented oasis. Hokum but no pokum.

W. F. N. WATSON

The Shoemakers' Holiday: Costume comedy about the apprentice of shoemaker who becomes Lord Mayor of London. A load of old cobblers!

BRENDAN GORSE

Ghosts: Young Norwegian does his nut after contracting unmentionable disease. Claptrap.

NAOMI MARKS

Death in Venice: Author fancies boy, catches bug. *Don't* take me to your Lido!

C. VITA-FINZI

Edward II: Gay king gets his come-uppance. Will keep you glued to your seat!

N. R. CARNE

The Young Churchill: Harrowing adventures and a bit of a Boer, but still the greatest Tory ever sold.

B. BALDWIN

The Ancient Mariner: Romantic reminiscences of an old sea dog (including how he got the bird). His blight proves to be worse than his barque.

R. INGHAM

Bicycle Thieves: Famous postwar neo-realist free-wheeler shows how De Bicycle Loser becomes De Sica. Some marvellous clips.

Klute: Involved *Psycho*thriller unravellable only by mensa minds. All very Pakula.

MOLLY FITTON

BLACK MISCHIEF

If General Amin visited England, presumably one of the royal family would be obliged to show him round. Competitors gladly depicted the scene.

Wa's dat?

The Tower of London, Mr – er – President.

Just call me General, Charlie. So, dat's where you keep 'em before the executions.

Executions, General?

Hangin', drawin' an' quarterin'. Beheadin'.

One is not aware of any executions in this country.

I get yuh! On the quiet! Say, who was the fat creep with the pipe at the airport?

You may be referring to the Prime Minister.

So what happened to the last one? Heath?

I believe he resigned. When one is born into my position, General, one does not discuss politics.

He's in dat Tower place?

Mr Heath? No, of course not.

Gone already! You boys sure work fast.

J. TIMSON

Ballater Station. August.

I'm Snowdon.

Yes – and ah'm Kilimanjaro.

That's bad enough for *Punch*.

You know Alan Coren?

Actually, no.

I meet him, I chop his balls off.

Indeed?

Fry 'em and eat 'em. Who this fat woman?

She's Maggie.

Ah can *see* she's baggy, man. But that's how ah like 'em – baggy, not scraggy.

Who is this ghastly little man, Tony?

This is the President.

Good God! Whatever happened to Ford? Or is this Nixon with a face-lift and a sun-tan?

You could say that.

And what part of Mississippi do *you* come from, my good man?

You's Mrs Sippy – ah's Mr Sappy.

You see, dear, the General is by way of being an entertainer as well.

But I thought it was *next* summer we were having the Black and White Minstrels at Balmoral. Still, now he's here, I suppose we can get him on to a bit of weeding . . .

RUFUS STONE

MRS. BEENDONEBY

Following the publication of Charles Kingsley's candid letters to his wife, competitors were invited to restore expurgated passages to any of his works.

Tom was rather disappointed with his gorse-and-thistle shirt. At first it was lovely and prickly and tickly and tormenting but, saturated with sea-water, it grew less and less itchy and irritating – which, of course, made poor Tom more and more irrita*ted*! However, there was always the weekly visit of Mrs Be-done-by-as-you-did – and her thrillingly swishy birch-rod! – to look forward to. For, truth to tell, Tom not only enjoyed being naughty but, in a queer sort of way, enjoyed being punished for his naughtiness. So this week he took pains to be *really* bad, cramming extra large stones as false dinners into the poor anemones' mouths, and tickling the corals almost to death. By behaving thus, Tom knew he would be assured of a really sound whipping – and of a nice warm tingly bottom, whose roseate blush he could admire in his own little mother-of-pearl sea-mirror . . .

Tim O'Dowda

When every breast is firm, lad,
And all the girls are keen;
And all their thighs are warm, lad,
And all that lies between:
Then ho! for wanton sport, lad,
And pleasure in the hay;
A hundred may you court, lad,
Before your wedding day.
When limb and lust are limp, lad,
And all your loves are old;
When breasts you held are spent, lad,
And once-warm thighs are cold;
See, through the autumn mist there,
Young lovers take your place;
Yet know you too once kissed there,
– Old age is no disgrace.

B. J. TICKLE

Under the snow-white coverlet, upon the snow-white pillow, lay the most beautiful little girl Tom had ever seen. Tom glanced back at the grimy reflection in the mirror. Should he wash first? But no: it was the soot in the creases that smarted so deliciously. He tiptoed across to the bed.

Falling on his knees (for you must know, children, that poor Tom, being only a poor little heathen, knew no better use for them), he looked up at the picture of the Man in the long garments, and it seemed to him that the Man smiled at him approvingly. Stretching out a hand, he touched her, as low as he dared.

Up jumped the little white lady in her bed, and, seeing Tom, screamed as shrill as any peacock.

'Don't be frightened!' pleaded poor Tom: 'I don't want to hurt you. I want *you* to hurt *me*.'

E. M. E. WOOD

GRAVE MATTERS

Elegies to contemporary bigwigs in the style of any notoriously good-bad poet

For Ray Gunter, after William McGonagall

It was once said (I forget by whom)
             about the late Ray Gunter
That he looked as if he'd been
    designed as a sort of artisan Billy Bunter:
An observation that you might well
             like to ponder –
Though, on the other hand, you might
          well not, I shouldn't wonder.
He made his name at a Labour Party Annual
    Conference with an impassioned oration
That made what one can only describe
         as a very mild sensation.
Some auditors even went so far as to
        call it a *tour de force*:
Certainly, when he eventually sat down,
        his throat was very hoarse –
Not that ending up with a throat that's hoarse
    is necessarily the test of a *tour de force*,
             of course!
Later on, there was increasingly something
         in the nature of a divorce
Between him and his fellow members
    because of his obsessive concentration
On the threat to British Industry of
        Bolshevik infiltration . . .

SIMON LITTIMER

For Mrs Thatcher, after Alfred Austin

Across the wires the electric message sped,
She is no better, actually, she's dead.
Fair Leaderette! with Party cares o'erladen,
Supreme example of a self-made maiden,
A grocer's daughter, born in Grantham, Lincs,
She got a Second in what some call 'Stinks',
But First in the affections of the Tories,
Secure in History she evermore is.
Though Number Ten she never dwelt inside,
Be sure the Pearly Gates will open wide
To welcome her, in heav'nly twin-set clad,
The best Prime Minister we never had.

STANLEY J. SHARPLESS

LITERARY LIMERICKS

Plots of various classics encapsulated in a limerick

Prince Hamlet thought Uncle a traitor
For having it off with his Mater;
    Revenge Dad or not?
    That's the gist of the plot,
And he did – nine soliloquies later.

STANLEY J. SHARPLESS

Black brasshat, suspected magician,
Gets spliced to Venetian patrician;
    But falls in the trap a
    Malign understrapper
Has covertly wrought for their fission.

COLIN KIMBERLEY

The Gamekeeper of Lady Chatterley
Was rewarded more often than qua'terly:
    'Though I feel quite a beast,'
    She reflected, 'at least
Now I'm having it off more than latterly.'

GERRY HAMILL

A man called Andronicus (Titus)
Had a nasty attack of colitis;
    It began with meat pies
    And the issuing cries
Of his sons saying, 'Daddy don't bite us!'

PAUL WIGMORE

Mr Rochester's wife's pyromania
Made him hanker for someone unzanier.
    'No, no!' said the parson.
    But, after more arson,
A little voice whispered: 'It's Jane here!'

GINA BERKELEY

ON THE WRONG SHELF

Competitors were asked to review or compose blurbs for books whose categories they had misunderstood

The Bible

Now you too can acquire an unexpurgated copy of this all-time best-seller. No nonsense with the prudish 'revised' version, for here with all its astonishingly outspoken frankness you get every word of the original with its thousand-and-one saucy tales of love, lust and violence, set in the torrid deserts and romantic sheikhdoms of the oil-rich Middle East. You've heard of Adam 'n' Eve? Now relish their strange and shameful story in all its amazing details! Learn of the unusual 'friendship' between a king, David, and young attractive Jonathan! Of Onan and the deed they still dare not name! Of the Hittites whose violence makes today's Mafia sound like a vicar's tea party! Keen on folk songs? Then why not learn to croon your favourite psalm (pronounce it *sarm*) but – our advice – *don't* start with the 119th! At no extra cost we include the, even by today's permissive standards, almost incredible acts of the apostles. But we're not going to spoil your excitement with the last chapter by revealing a thing about those truly fantastic Revelations!

DOUGLAS GAIRDNER

Inside Number 10

Yet another romantic novel in well-worn tradition of Cartland and Robbins. Humble young secretary works for dashing handsome boss who is greying at the temples (he even has a wife who writes poetry). There are numerous minor villains, lurking mandarins of the civil service. But the background is unconvincing. Could a man like this ever become a prime minister? Not in *my* book. And the rest of the cabinet are equally unconvincing. After all, they are supposed to be a Labour government, but behave like Tories. The plot is all too predictable and set me wondering if Marcia Williams could even be the mink-and-diamonds Barbara, except for the unhappy ending when the poor secretary finishes up on the slag-heap.

M. K. CHEESEMAN

Crockford's Clerical Directory

This definitive work could be described as the male counterpart to the ill-fated *Ladies Directory* which, nevertheless, in its brief existence, managed to bring so much solace into the lives of so many people. The nation-wide network of male persons registered here are all anxious to offer their ministrations (usually *gratis*, though for some services there is a small nominal charge) to all those in need of them. A simple code reveals the range of services available. 'Deacon' or 'Curate' is for beginners; 'Vicar' or 'Rector' for the more experienced; 'Archdeacon' for the more proficient yet; 'Dean' for the really advanced – though only full-blown 'Bishops' are licensed to go the whole hog. You need never be lonely with a copy of Crockford.

KIT CARPENTER

The London Telephone Directory

At last a great literary masterpiece *de nos jours* which bears comparison with Dickens, Jane Austen, George Eliot, Hardy and other giants of the past. Breathtaking in concept, astonishing in its observation and unflagging attention to detail, this story of life in the metropolis leaves the reader stunned by the sheer energy that must have gone into its making. The style is sparse to the point of childlike simplicity, yet the very suppression of emotion gives the book an overpowering impact. The well-plotted novel has long been out of fashion, but here there is virtually no storyline at all. But what a range of characters! The reader will be held from the stark opening – '1-2-3 Express Typing Service' – to the final doomladen sentence: 'Zyxomma Information Enterprises . . .'

F. R. VESS

THE ODD COUPLE

The devil damn thee black, thou creamfaced loon,
Whom we invite to see us crowned at Scone

Competitors yoked similarly strange poetic bedfellows to form a couplet.

Walking from watch to watch, from
                     tent to tent
A sort of naughty persons, lewdly bent.
               (*HV/HIV, 2*)

J. H. BENTLEY

Then up he rose and donned his clothes –
We scorn her most when most she
           offers blows (*Hamlet/A & C*)

GERRY HAMILL

Endymion sought around, and shook
                 each bed
I left poor Scylla in a niche and fled.
             (Keats: *Endymion*)

B. K. BRINTON

And flights of angels sing thee to thy rest
A couch for luxury and damned incest.
                 (*Hamlet*)

JANET I. HARRIS

Eros! I come, my queen – Eros! Stay for me!
Then slip I from her bum – down
           topples she. (*A&C/MND*)

P. W. R. FOOT

Please it your Holiness, I think it be
Thou art too ugly to attend on me
          (Marlowe: *Doctor Faustus*)

JOHN WILLIAMS

Come, we'll to sleep. My strange
              and self-abuse
Is the initiate fear that wants hard use.
               (*Macbeth*)

T. GRIFFITHS

Friends, Romans, countrymen – lend me
              your ears
Make your two eyes, like stars, start from
         their spheres. (*J.C./Hamlet*)

BELINDA GAMMON

Oh what a rogue and peasant slave am I!
Why, 'tis a loving and a fair reply. (*Hamlet*)

H. A. C. EVANS

She knows the heat of a luxurious bed
Gets him to rest cramm'd with
        distressful bread. (*Much Ado/Henry V*)

TOM BREWER

A little touch of Harry in the night,
Put out the light, and then put out
         the light. (*Henry V/Othello*)

J. A. GAMMON

I conjure thee, by Rosaline's fair thigh,
Stray lower, where the pleasant
        fountains lie. (*R. & J./Venus & Adonis*)

ADAM KHAN

VEG. PROG. COUP.
WISH SHARE BUNG.

**Competitors submitted gruesomely uninviting small-ads,
under Personal, Accommodation, etc.**

Personalise your protectives! True Togetherness condemns the *anonymous* condom – for Beautiful People are Sharing People – they like to give meaningfulness to their Love-Making by the added magic of naming. And what more tender and intimate mode of identity-sharing could you find than asking us to print your name (not *nom d'amour*) in tasteful lettering (fluorescent for convenience in the dark) on your own deeply sincere set of individualised sheaths. So – make your every orgasm a 'studded' success!

The Ramaswamimurtikrivenatajmahala Memorial Hall and Meditation Centre. Yogosakitiguri Homashimawawawawa on 'The Meaninglessness of Nothing'. All welc.

CHESTER FIELD

Halitosis? Acne? Dandruff? Send s.a.e. for free samples.

I. C. SNELL

Pock-marked, colour blind lady of melancholy temperament, fattish legs and suffering from halitosis would like to meet similar male interested in ghouls and diseases of the scalp; preferably heavy smoker and tone deaf.

STEPHEN CORRIN

Unrecognised genius, 65, inventor, writer, painter, sculptor, trumpet-player, will exchange lifetime's papers, MSS, canvases, bronzes (some large) for own room and meals *en famille*, central London.

HENRY TUBE

Holiday with a Meths Drinker's Commune in Plaistow. Debs and Dolly Birds welcome. Lots of unusual entertainment. Abasement of social workers; Bottling, Butting and Biting contests, etc. Advance booking to Groper George (with ten pound note), under Waterloo Bridge. No credit cards please.

RUSSELL LUCAS

LITTLE BOY GREENE

Nursery rhymes rewritten in the style of modern novelists

'Jack Sprat' after Hemingway

'Come in, Jack.'
'I d'wanta come in.'
'D'wanta come in, hell. Come in bright boy.'
They went in.
'I'll have eats now,' she said. She was fat and red.
'I'd want nothing,' Jack said. He was thin and pale.
'D'want nothin' hell. You have eats now, bright boy.'
She called the waiter. 'Bud,' she said, 'gimme bacon and beans – twice.'
Bud brought the bacon and beans.
'I d'want bacon. It's too fat,' said Jack.
'D'want bacon, hell. I'll eat the fat. You eat the lean. OK big boy?'
'OK,' Jack said.
They had eats.
'Now lick the plate clean,' she said.
'Aw, honey,' said Jack, 'I aint gotta, do I?'
'Yup,' she said. 'You gotta.'
They both licked their plates clean.

HENRY HETHERINGTON

'Little Jack Horner' after Anthony Powell

Horner had got himself established as far as possible from the centre of the room and I was suddenly made aware, as one often is by actions which are in themselves quite commonplace, that he was about to do something which would give him enormous satisfaction. He had somehow acquired a large seasonal confection which he was beginning to attack with a degree of enthusiasm I had not seen him display since the midnight feasts we had enjoyed at school. Eschewing the normal recourse to eating utensils, he plunged his hand through the pastry and extracted an entire fruit, an achievement which was accompanied by a cry of self-congratulation and a beatific expression reminiscent of some of those on the faces one sees in the more popular of the Pre-Raphaelite portraits.

ALAN ALEXANDER

'Solomon Grundy' after P. G. Wodehouse

It's odd how Dame Fortune (whom I sometimes suspect of being Aunt Agatha in drag) takes the most frightful scunner to some chappies. Take the case of little Sol Grundy, prize Drone and no slouch when it came to the festive bread-bunging. No sooner does the poor mutt get himself under starter's orders for the Life Stakes (with yours truly standing sponsor at the font) than he's spliced to the most god-awful girl east of Esher. Then, before you can say 'Man Friday', he's wrapped his lungs round some bacillus of no fixed address, starts going downhill with the speed of a welshing bookie and – hey presto! – 24 hours later, he's shuffled off this mortal whatsit and is pushing up the dandelions. As Jeeves remarked: 'Here today – gone yesterday' – or words to that effect. Smart cove, Jeeves.

KIT CARPENTER

MY WIFE AND I

Extracts from Mr Thatcher's Diary or samples from his forthcoming collection of verse

The telephone goes ting-a-ling again,
That's ten bloody calls in an hour.
'I'll ask her to give you a ring' again,
'That's rather a personal thing' again,
'She'd *love* to address you in Tring' again,
Who *wants* the clap-trappings of power?

The washing machine's on the blink again,
The whole bloody house is a mess.
The fridge is beginning to stink again,
The dishes are piled in the sink again,
'Yes, *doesn't* she look in the pink' again,
What price the bitch-goddess success?

GERRY HAMILL

Awoke 6 a.m. Megs already scratching away at her escritoire – had conceived three brilliant new platitudes in the small hours, and was incorping them into the speech she is to deliver to the YC of Bletchley, the WI of Dungeness and the OAP of Llanelli. Say one thing for Megs, she never says the same thing once. Will have to get about a bit in the next few days if I'm to get any slap-and-tickle; she has a very tight schedule (that's a new word for it, ha ha).

I. C. SNELL

Ankle damaged in vaulting over wire fence to escape newsmen still painful. Said to Maggie: 'If this *tendon*cy continues, I shall need some more a-*sprains*!' How we roared! the closer you get to the top, the more you need a sense of humour.

IAN KELSO

DON'T BOTHER TO WRITE

It was felt that the Arts Council, far from subsidising new talent, should pay would-be literati *not* to write their books. Sample first pages of these doomed works were provided.

Upsy and Daisy

'Women are quite unfathomable,' asseverated Father.

Happily Uncle Edgar was up to form. 'I would agree with that,' riposted he, 'were it not that, in looking into their depths, it is always so confoundedly easy to glimpse their bottoms.'

When the laughter had finally died:

'Full fathom five our uncle *lies*,' trilled my adorable twin, Daisy, misquoting aptly, and flashing her dangerous gypsy beauty straight at me. I flashed back my own (we were identical twins) and my 18-year-old hand groped for hers, found it warm and unresisting.

TERENCE RATTIGAN

A Simple Life

I have always written briefly of the very
                  simple things –
Springtime flowers and Autumn colours,
           kittens' fur and bluebirds' wings.
But this world is wide, and little things add
               up to something great
All those brief and fleeting moments weave
            the pattern of our Fate.
So I wish to tell the story of my uneventful
                     life
As I grew from Child to Woman, playful
            Babe to loving Wife,
Now at last to Great-Great-Granny, birth
          to tranquil age and strength,
For my story is a woman's, epic only in its
                 length.
I was born to simple parents in a cosy
            bungalow:
Number 5, Laburnum Villas, just one
          hundred years ago . . .

ANN HARTLAND-SWANN

GIVE ME YOUR ANSWER DO

**Was the Shakespearean sonneteering one-sided, or did the
Fair Youth and Dark Lady reply in kind? They did.**

In Reply to Sonnet 149

You call it love? You must be jesting, mate –
My mother did not bear me yesterday.
I am no blushing pink computer-date:
I'm on the game that only two can play.
Poor mixed-up poet – in your belfry-tower
The flittermice are flying round and round –
Keep your endearments for the perfect flower
Of womanhood, if such is to be found.
The popsies in your plays are rosy-lipped
But only figments of your fantasy:
No way you'll make it with a manuscript
In quite the style you're making it with me.
I once was pure. It was before the Flood.
But pure or poxed, Will – I am flesh
                        and blood!

STANLEY SHAW

Hello dere Will, an' t'ank you for de pome.
For l'il ol' me, it was a big surprise
To find it waitin' here when I got home,
An' all dose words sho' opened up my eyes
To t'ings about myself I hadn't thought.
An' now I'm readin' some de lines agin,
I'm t'inkin' you got funny ways to court,
An' ought to mind more 'bout what you sayin'.
What all dis 'black wires' and breath
                              dat's smelly
An' writin' 'bout de colour o' my breast?
You din't say dat when perchin' on my belly
An' pantin' away in yo' dirty vest.
If yo' nex' words doan make some
                              sweeter noise,
You'd better stick to makin' frien's wid boys.

MARTIN SHERWOOD

Shall I compare thee to an actor? – no!
Thou art more wooden than the boards you
                              tread;
Your windmill rantings do annoy me so
I wish thy Globe-girt motley swiftly shed.
Thy verses limp like cripples, lacking feet;
You do advise me, and yet lack all sense;
What other poets say I daren't repeat;
I still do scorn thee and do bid thee hence.
We met upon an evening, long ago since past;
You caught my sleeve and were importunate,
A play went forth – we were the only cast –
One act, not five, and ending with a mate.
Since then you've plied me with your
                              wordy stuff,
So once again, I say I've had enough.

MAUD GRACECHURCH

THANKSGIVINGS

Events and customs for the annual celebration of any twentieth-century British poet

The Patience Strong Afternoon

A stroll thro' a cottage garden to gather fragrant roses; and pluck from the hedgerows of time sweet memories' dainty posies; then a walk through the village churchyard while we think of departed friends, steeping ourselves in that peace of soul that dear remembrance lends; then striding across the moors to gaze on the rugged fells, as we hark to the curlew's wistful cry and distant wind-blown bells; then sauntering thro' the twilit woods or by the winding stream, attuned to nature's mystic lore, that magic realm of dream. Then back through the fields, the shining grass with the dews of evening lacquered – and into the 'Fleece' for a triple gin, for after all that we'll be knackered.

MOLLY FITTON

Visitors to the Hardy Festival should take the midnight train on the old Great Western line, changing at Westbury for Dorchester West. The Festival Committee will be waiting to welcome them at Dorchester South. A short reception to meet local ruined maids will be held in the Journeying Boy Bar of the Max Gate Motel. Then a visit to the Dorchester workhouse, and related-interest trips to Wessex Heights 'n Sights. Then two lectures at the Museum; 'Hardy's Finances' will consider Hardy's view that verse paid better than prose, and J. Stephens Cox will reveal 'What Hardy got in his Eye in Lyonesse'. The Memorial Dinner will not be held, as all the invitations will have gone astray. Finally the party will forgather at the grave of the cat, which, according to the late Bishop of Worcester, consumed Hardy's heart in the left-luggage room at Sturminster Newton station.

TONY LURCOCK

The central event of any Kingsley Amis Night is the ritual burning on a bonfire of a 'Leftie'. Effigies are normally those of any stereotype 'Weirdie Beardie', but can be made in the likeness of any real-life 'Leftie' who is the target of right-wing attacks of the moment. Use firelighters made of the *Morning Star*, *Tribune*, *New Statesman* etc., for lighting the fire. Before being placed on the pyre, the effigy is solemnly processed around it, as 'The Red Flag' is chanted *backwards*, as a mark of disrespect. This is similar to the reciting of the Lord's Prayer backwards in the Black Mass. As the bonfire is lit, guests hurl on to it trade union membership cards, left-wing books, etc., while muttering suitable curses. Sherry or madeira and biscuits are then partaken of.

HARRISON EVERARD

MORE BAWLS

Coarse songs for unlikely games

We played a game of chess in bed,
And this is what my girlfriend said:

Why flog your Bishop for a Knight?
That was a silly thing to do.
If you'd mounted an attack,
You'd have had me on my back
And you could have forced a mate in two.
What made you think I would resist?
You could have really swept the floor.
What a bloody silly move,
And it only goes to prove
That you don't know what your piece is for!

NAOMI MARKS

Of all the pieces that I've played
  There's none like lovely Rita.
I love to play her Opening
  No gambit could be neater.

She is positionally strong
  She knows the variations,
But most of all I like to see
  Her pretty combinations.

I tried to fork her one black night
  But I miscalculated;
She niftily unpinned herself
  And thus she got me mated.

JEDEDIAH BARROW

Oh, Three won't do, and Five won't do,
Four it's got to be!
Take my wife, and I'll take yours;
They'll lap it up, you'll see!

Oh, yours can play, and mine can play:
You'll find she understands!
Conventions never trouble her.
She's dandy with her hands!

Oh, let's begin, and no holds barred,
There's liquor in the fridge.
The kids are out, so let's enjoy
A cosy game of bridge.

W.S.B.

MY MISTAKE

**Competitors were asked to insert creative compositorial
errors into well-known lines.**

When Kempenfelt went down
On twice four hundred men. (Cowper)

ANNE B. RODGERS

This is the way the world ends
Not with a bang but a wimpy.

DORIS PULSFORD

Rough winds do shake the darling
bubs of May.

TONY LURCOCK

Some mute inglorious Hilton here may rest.

D. H. CROWN

She stood in tears amid the alien porn.

GEORGE HURREN

Beneath the rule of men entirely great
The penis mightier than the sword.
(Bulwer-Lytton)

STEPHEN CORRIN

Hoover through the fog and filthy air.

D. SMITH

There's a breathless lush in the
Close tonight. (Newbolt)

COLIN KIMBERLEY

To muse and brood and live again
in memory,
With those old faeces of our infancy.
(Tennyson)

JETHRO B. TUCKET

An enema hath done this. (St Matthew)

L. REEVE JONES

And may there be no moaning at the bar
When I send out for tea.

EVE GAMMON

Stood Dido with a willy in her hand.

T. A. DYER

PING PONGS

A recent visitor to a Chinese school heard a three-year-old denouncing Teng Hsiao-ping, a freshly disgraced figure. A similar *j'accuse* came from an English tot.

Poo to Mister Benn . . . Poo Poo to his terrible fibs and horrid speeches. We don't want his nasty Labourites with their tatty red flags . . . creeping down our lane.

We don't want their rotten old council-houses near our paddock. Poo to all his lazy bingo-playing slackers who are ruining this country and filling it with smelly foreigners and really mucky trade-unionists. There wouldn't be enough room to gallop our horses, or even my little pony, if they all came here.

If everybody worked as hard as Daddy does at Slater Walker, England would be a super place. We believe in freedom and Aunty Thatcher, who talks like Nanny and doesn't wee her knickers or suck her thumb. Mister Benn does . . . So POO.

RUSSELL LUCAS

LASCIVIOUS EVERY EVENING DESPITE SENILITY

NORWICH at the foot of a love letter signifies Nickers Off Ready When I Come Home. Competitors provided more acronyms for itinerant randies.

LLANFAIR . . . GOGOGOCH

Linking Letters And Names Fosters Acrostic Indelicacy. Regular Prize Winners Like Literary Goals, Whereas Yahoos Now Grab Your Lousy Loot, Gorged On Geographically-Expressed Rudery. Your Competition Humours Warped Readers' Nastier Drolleries. Remember, Obscenity Begets Wantonness, Lechery, Lewdness, Lasciviousness, Lubricity And Naughty Things (Including Sex – I Loathe It). Obscene Gags Or Giggles Often Give Older Competitors Hiccups.

J. M. HAYNES

Listen Lovely Accountancy's No Fun Actually I Really Prefer Women Long Legs Great Wet Yearning Nipples Gorgeous Yawning Luscious Lips Getting Old George Excited . . . Right You Corker Here's What You Really Need Don't Rush Ouch Bloody Wait Listen Later La . . . Lower Aaaah Now Then Yes Steady I Listen I Oh God Oh God Ooh God! Oooh CHRIST! ! Hankie?

J. ARTHUR RIDDLE

WINDSOR

When I'm Near, Darling, Strip Off Regalia.

MICHAEL WEST

SWANSEA

Say When Available – No Spouse Etcetera About.

L. G. UDALL

CHELTENHAM

Colonels Here Expect Lovemaking Twice Every Night. Hurry Aunt Mabel!

BATH

Bedsprings Always Twang Harmoniously.

GLYNDBOURNE

Got Lustful Young Nymphet Decidedly Behind Orchestra – Unusual Repertoire Neatly Executed.

JOHN MUIRHEAD

WARMINSTER

Will Assert Rights, Madge, If 'No Sex Tonight' Expostulation Repeated.

STANLEY J. SHARPLESS

VIRGINIA WATER

Vital Inflate Rubber Girl Immediately No Intercourse Available Without Astronomical Tariff En Route.

PADDY BEESLEY

EDINBURGH

Erection Definitely Imminent Now. Book Usual Room Grand Hotel.

BRENDON GORSE

NO BALLS

As I was going to St Pauls
A lady grabbed me by the elbow . . .
Competitors provided more lines in this regrettable vein.

I dreamed I dwelt in marble halls
Of ample airs and sumptuous tinge,
While odalisques caressed my cheeks,
Each with a moist and willing palm.

I dreamed I sauntered on the front
At Cannes, where I had moored my yacht.
The movie stars! The lavish cars!
The fine display of Gallic charm!

I dreamed I discoed at the Ritz –
The evening warm, the music cool –
And gorgeous girls who tossed their curls
Admired my sleek and well-hung clothes.

But then I woke, and cursed my luck;
My heart relapsed, my spirits sank.
No yacht in France, no girls, no dance –
No option but to have a doze.

BASIL RANSOME

As I was going to Saint Paul's
A lady took me by the Ball's
Pond Road, to see if I would care
Just to go and see her bare
Her soul down at the New Sugawn
(A pub where you can get the Horn
Of plenty in the way of drama);
I thought that I would have to ram her
Through the crowd to get her in
To the place where she would scin-
Tillate till ten, or thereabouts
(After a few I had my doubts).
And then it came from out her stock –
About the most enormous Cock
And Bull Tale heard, it made me vexed . . .
(To be continued in our next).

                    BILL MANLEY

If you can ride the storm aboard a lugger,
    And bravely manage in the wind to spit;
If you can hold your own against a head-wind,
    And laugh to find yourself knee-deep
                                in spray;

If you can face the mighty ocean's bucking,
    And fix your eyes unswerving to the front;
If you can stand all night and keep on compass,
    And still have strength enough for one
                            more watch;

If you can laugh at Fate, the Gods ignoring,
    And keep a steady course between the rocks;
If all your days and nights are spent in sailing –
    The chances are, you'll end up with the first
            prize in the *Observer* single-handed
                    Transatlantic Race.

                    ALBAN GIRRAL

DOG EATS DOG

**Competitors devised clerihews on regular contributors to the
NS – including, of course, their excellent selves**

St Mug,
Bitten by a pessimystic bug,
Thinks ours will be the fate of Sodom
                              and Gomorrah
Tomorrah.

Hopefully, Kingsley Amis
Won't see this,
Else there'd be a confrontation
Situation.

                              STANLEY J. SHARPLESS

Richard Noakes
Is one of those blokes
Who, though he has not yet won,
Thinks he ought to have done.

                              RICHARD NOAKES

Paul Theroux
Writes about new books.
(Or is it pronounced Therou?
In which case he writes about books that
                              are new.

                              C. VITA-FINZI

Mr Anthony Howard,
Though intellectually high-powered,
Finds themes couldn't be elusiver
When he's doing Crucifer.

                              S. A. PRIDDLE

Mr Martin Fagg
Isn't one to brag,
But keeps a teeny weeny list
Of entries that missed.

                              DAN HAZLEWOOD

When offered the job of TV critic,
Dennis Potter
Exclaimed: 'What a
Wonderful chance to write about the only
                              thing that interests me –
I.e. Potter, D.'

'Shucks!'
Cried Anthony Howard when told
                              that 'Crux'
Was no longer available. There's no
                              excuse if a
Chap can't even think up a – I've got it! –
                              'Crucifer'!'

                              COLIN KIMBERLEY

As a poet, he may not be in
                              Elizabeth Barratt's
Class; but E. O. Parrott's
Competition entries certainly stand out from
                              the rest of the jetsam –
Particularly when he sets 'em.

                              ALBAN GIRRAL

Paul Johnson
After his *Staggers* swan-song,
Wrote a book which he hopes
Will be cash for old Popes.

                              MAUD GRACECHURCH

Assiac
Writes even briefer notes than Old Moore
                              in his Almanac;
But that's chess,
I guess.

                              JETHRO B. TUCKET

SOUNDS FAMILIAR

Synthetic poems, all of whose lines would already be familiar to any browser of Palgrave

The curfew tolls the knell of parting day;
The hungry sheep look up and are not fed;
Ill fares the land, to hastening ills a prey;
I would that I were dead.

O dark, dark, dark amid the blaze of noon
I heard a voice within the tavern cry
'The world is too much with us, late and soon,
And when we drink, we die.'

The time is out of joint; O cursed spite!
Toil, envy, want, the patron and the jail
In the wide womb of uncreated night –
I die! I faint! I fail!

BASIL RANSOME

When lovely woman stoops to folly
In the happy fields of hay,
Then heigh-ho, the holly; this life is most jolly,
Gather ye rosebuds while ye may.
My heart leaps up when I behold
Thy long-preserved virginity;
Bring me my arrows of desire,
Because my love has come to me.
Let us go then, you and I,
Under the wide and starry sky,
We'll tak' a cup o' kindness yet,
Lest we forget, lest we forget.

S. J. KILMINGTON

When in disgrace with fortune and men's eyes,
I stood in Venice on the Bridge of Sighs;
Then I felt like some watcher of the skies,
When youth grows spectre-thin and dies.
Stop and consider; life is but a day,
A dupe and a deceiver; a decay,
When I perhaps compounded am with clay,
And fools who came to scoff, remained to pray.
Visions of glory spare my aching sight,
One truth is clear, whatever is, is right.

ANDREW PAUL

INACTIVITIES

The 'men of action' who choose records on a BBC radio programme tend to be vice-chancellors, civil servants, etc. Competitors were asked to describe a day in the life of one of these worthies in the style associated with more obvious action-men.

At nine I kicked the door open and went in, fast. They were waiting. The meeting lasted four hours, one used by me to blast the Deans on admissions. Nobody yelled at me. Lunch was a sandwich, a flat pint and the mail, in my office. At two the call came. I made London by three, found the UGC man waiting and told him so he'd stay told. His teeth chattered. Gloria said no dice as I left. The Whitehall mob at the Bridges (Dental) Inquiry didn't like what I told them. I wrote my report while they said so. I headed for home, ate supper over a chess problem and the estimates. Then to bed with the Rothschild Report. I didn't need any barbiturates.

PETER ALEXANDER

The Borough Treasurer looked at his wife, still asleep in bed. She had the kind of gritty female-ness he found irresistible; it's not every woman who runs a playgroup, he reflected.

    After dressing, he sprinted downstairs and wolfed a plate of Shreddies in one minute flat. Grabbing his executive briefcase, he ran to his Morris 1100 and leapt in. As he turned the ignition key, the engine roared on full choke. Within minutes he was cruising into his reserved parking space at the Town Hall. Life is good, he thought; very good. It's not every man who sits all day on a million pounds of ratepayers' money. And weren't the Masons making their customary clandestine approaches? 'Icing on the cake,' he chuckled, and in that moment the little finger of his right hand crooked involuntarily.

TIM HOPKINS

JUST WHAT I WANTED

Truly up-to-the-minute shopping lists for the twelve days of Christmas, the second prize-winner providing an, apparently, genuine Hawaiian version

On the twelfth day of Christmas
My true love sent to me:
Twelve nymphos mating,
Eleven virgins waiting,
Ten colonels spanking,
Nine schoolboys cranking,
Eight nuns assenting,
Seven monks repenting,
Six queers consenting,
Five dutch caps;
Four birth pills,
Three condoms,
Two IUDs,
And a call girl calling on me.

TIM HOPKINS

Numba Twelve Day of Christmas
My Tutu give to me:
Twelve television,
Eleven missionary,
Ten can of beer,
Nine pound of poy,
Eight ukelele,
Seven shrimp a-swimming,
Six hula lesson,
Five big fat pig;
Four flower lei,
Three dry squid,
Two coconut,
And a minah bird in a papaya tree.

LISELOTTE LESCHKE

On the twelfth day of Christmas
My true love sent to me:
Twelve grumblers grumbling,
Eleven strikers striking,
Ten widows weeping,
Nine bombers blasting,
Eight traders bilking,
Seven statesmen trimming,
Six parsons praying,
Five last flings;
Four bawling kids,
Three wet beds,
Two words of love,
And an overpriced, underhung Tree.

MARY HOLTBY

WAKEY WAKEY

Extracts from *The Butlin Archipelago*, **etc.**

'Strip'. Steven Cecilovitch Carstairs shuddered. The unventilated and overcrowded cattle plane, the endless wait at the arrival point where incomprehensible announcements had shattered every attempt at sleep, the first sight of the shabby and rickety huts, had still not prepared him for what was regarded by inmates with even greater loathing than the plastic tokens by which they measured their place in the pecking-order of the pig troughs: the animal nakedness that is the uniform of the *Clubmed*.

He stripped. The Mars Bar he had recklessly concealed in his hernia belt thudded to the ground. A whisper, louder than any screaming, stunned him; in an instant he was awash in a whirlpool of bodies scratching, kicking, biting . . .

C. VITA-FINZI

On the second morning I looked out for Smithsov. He was sitting at a table, practising bingo calls for the afternoon's Group Elation Treatment. With tears in my eyes I approached him. 'Tell me, Smithsov. Is it true that a man can't be unhappy here?'

'Brownsov,' he replied with compassion in his voice. 'Unhappiness does not exist.' As he spoke, the Chief Redcoat roared from the end of the ward: 'Everybody happy?'

'Yes!' screamed the patients in unison. I glanced at Smithsov for reassurance and as I did so, his bowtie lit up and began to revolve at great speed. Simultaneously, the flower in his buttonhole squirted water in my face.

'Everybody happy?' I reflected. 'Of course we are.'

TIM HOPKINS

UNGLAMOROUS KNIGHT

Where are they now? A Shakespearean character in 1976

Falstaff

Eamonn wants me on. Yes, but how if Eamonn wants me off when I
come on? – how then? Can Eamonn get me a keg? No. Or a bird? No.
Or take away a primary chancre? No. Eamonn hath no skill in treating
social diseases, then? No. What is Eamonn? A star. What maketh him to
shine? An autocue. *This Is Your Life* – who watches it? He that hath
naught else to do o'Wednesday. Do we need it? No. Can we bear it?
No. It is mindless crap, then? Yea, to all but the dead. But will it not
entertain the living? No. Why? Self-respect will not suffer it. Therefore
I'll none of it; Eamonn is a pain in the arse; and so ends my contract.

F. R. VESS

No – I'm not prepared to say how much rake-off I get per man I enlist
for these foreign wars. That's a matter between me and the organisation –
question of professional integrity, old boy . . . Well, yes – I *am* the
organisation – but the principle's the same . . . Incidentally, it *is* understood
that you pick up the bill for this very handsome lunch *plus* the two
hundred quid your paper's paying for the interview? Good . . . Waiter –
another treble brandy – *pronto* . . . Yes, having a handle *does* still count
for something in England . . . Good thing too . . . Far too little attention
paid to blood and breeding these days . . . Precisely the kind of
qualities that Falstaff Security Services are trying to instil in these young
chaps we're sending out to Africa . . .

KIT CARPENTER

ASSORTED ANAGRAMS

**'Sir Gas Bag' happens to be an anagram of
Asa Briggs. More were asked for.**

Denis Healey: Enid Eyelash.

Lord Montgomery: God! Try Rommel On!

R. S. WILSON

Richard Ingrams, Auberon Waugh, Nigel Dempster:
Warning – Hard Men Harbour Grudges, Malice, Spite.

MIKE DAUB

Marcia, Lady Falkender: Fancy Me, Lar-da-dar like!

ANTHONY JARVIS

Reginald Maudling: In a Glaring Muddle.

Harold Macmillan: I Charm All, Old Man.

DAVID PHILIPS

Iris Murdoch: Horrid Music.

Simon Raven: Rains Venom.

EMMA FISHER

Michelangelo Buonarroti: A mural, one ceiling, or both?

Florence Nightingale: Fight gore! Clean linen!

JOYCE JOHNSON

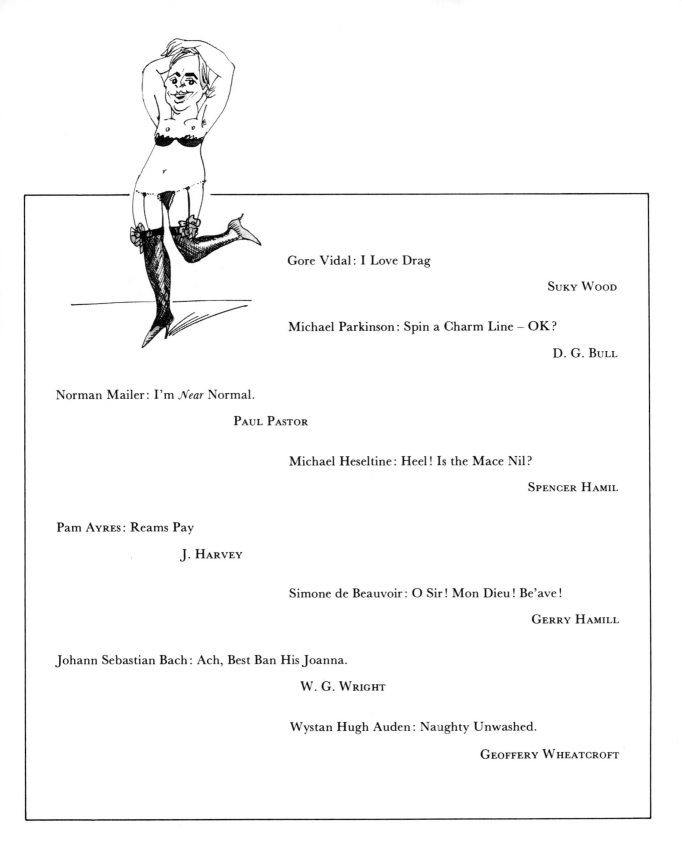

Gore Vidal: I Love Drag

SUKY WOOD

Michael Parkinson: Spin a Charm Line – OK?

D. G. BULL

Norman Mailer: I'm *Near* Normal.

PAUL PASTOR

Michael Heseltine: Heel! Is the Mace Nil?

SPENCER HAMIL

Pam AYRES: Reams Pay

J. HARVEY

Simone de Beauvoir: O Sir! Mon Dieu! Be'ave!

GERRY HAMILL

Johann Sebastian Bach: Ach, Best Ban His Joanna.

W. G. WRIGHT

Wystan Hugh Auden: Naughty Unwashed.

GEOFFERY WHEATCROFT

MORE FOUL FARE

**Competitors again devised disgusting meals, this time in verse,
moving smoothly from mackerel fool, conger-eel pasty, and beans
on stoat to gherkin sorbet and Steradent punch.**

Have some liquorice with your sherry,
While I dunk a pickled cherry
In the whisky we discovered in Cadiz.
Here's the entrée, nicely crusted
With a rich vanilla custard –
So you'd never guess there's
                   roll mops underneath!

Bet you didn't know that Betty,
Calls this 'A. A. Milne Spaghetti',
For she butters it with marmalade instead.
And we like our Stilton runny,
So we thin it out with honey –
You'll adore it on some steaming gingerbread.

Hope your tummy's nice and hollow –
There's a pudding still to follow:
It's a purée of banana and courgette.

Oh! You're tied up Monday lunchtime?
Never mind – there's Sunday brunch time;
There'll be cabbage juice, and poached
                   eggs vinaigrette!

NICK ENRIGHT

Cod-liver oil and Babycham will start the
                   meal of course,
And then Sheeps' Eyes in Aspic with tripe
                   and chocolate sauce,
Horse Liver braised in Marmite with Sardine
                   Dumplings (two)
And Aniseed Potatoes creamed with
                   tapioca chou,
Pigs' Trotters served in Advocaat and Curried
                   Jellied Eels,
A Claret Galantine wherein a Whole Sheep's
                   Brain congeals,
Then Sugared Onions, Treacled Eggs and
                   Toffee-Coated Peas,
And mentholated Coffee served with Peanut
                   Butter Cheese.

GERRY HAMILL

I'll start with Dubonnet and Coke,
Then, just as a bit of a joke,
Some gooseberry forcemeat
With finely chopped horsemeat
And *blanquette* of pig in a poke.

Next, raspberry-flavoured *pommes frites*,
Fried egg on choc-ice kedgeree,
A hole (without toad)
Marmalade *à la mode*,
Curried *café*. And *bon appetit*!

S. J. KILMINGTON

When we came in
It was yoghourt and gin,
Then a soup made of treacle and leeks.
Next a delicate dish
Syllabub (fish);
The wine had been open for weeks.

Two left in a hurry
At chocolate log curry,
And wine which we drank from a cup.
(Burgundy, red,
Or so our host said,
With some port in, to sweeten it up.)

The pudding we had
Was not quite so bad,
A compote of kippers and custard.
But best of the deal
Was the end of the meal,
An emetic of rock salt and mustard.

PHILIP MONTAGNON

UNHAPPILY EVER AFTER

Poems from Betjeman, or any previous Laureate, on what has been called 'the end of a fairy-tale romance'

After Betjeman

Princess Margaret Rose, Princess
                Margaret Rose,
How mad I was, sad I was, glad when
                you chose
A working photographer to be your mate:
What a lift for a lensman – oh, enviable fate!

How gracious, how spirited, how democratic
To form an alliance with an Instamatic!
But very soon after, tongues started to wag,
And others than Tony were seen in your Jag.

Now the romance is ended – no question,
                of course,
Of getting a common-or-garden divorce;
Darkroom widow, alone with your children
                and snaps,
The news-hounds will give you a break
                now, perhaps.

STANLEY J. SHARPLESS

After Alfred Austin

Upon my coloured screen, the bland
                announcers state:
'There won't be a divorce, but they
                will separate.'
And when one looks back fondly to the
                nuptials in the Abbey,
Such a very casual ending seems somehow
                rather shabby.
It grieves each loyal heart to see how Eros'
                whims dispose
Of her whom as a little girl we knew as
                'Margaret Rose'.
Her home-life has been most unlike that of
                her queenly sister;
And now, I fear, her future years present a
                dreary vista.
Unhappy chance did earlier, in the lists of
                Love, defeat her –
When Church and State prevented her from
                wedding gallant Peter.
But she, as well as lesser fry, may prove the
                third time lucky –
So keep your pecker up now, Ma'am, be
                resolute and plucky!

CLAUDE SPETTIGUE

After Betjeman

Peering at the pictures phoney,
Of her idyll with young Tony,
On the new expensive Sony,
   Sat Mrs Armstrong-Jones.
Wishing now that she were single
Able with the herd to mingle
Fancy-free and heart a-tingle,
   Was Mrs Armstrong-Jones.
So she asked her older sister
If she could discard her mister;
Now she's loose, but Lloyds still list her,
   As Mrs Armstrong-Jones.

JETHRO B. TUCKETT

After Masefield

I must go down to the seas again, to the warm
      and welcome isles,
For all I ask is a sweet relief from the cameras
      and the smiles,
From the bloody films and the gimlet eyes of
      the sycophantic types,
And the Daily this and the Sunday that with
      their moralising gripes.

I must go down to the seas again to escape
      from the dreary rounds
Of the duty lunch with the same old bunch and
      the same old horsey sounds,
For all I ask is a merry yarn from a laughing
      fellow rover,
And a quiet drink and a quiet sleep when the
      quiet day is over.

I must go down to the seas again, far from the
      fairly tale:
It's a wild call and a clear call, but it puts me
      beyond the pale.
When the Woman's this and the Woman's that
      have enjoyed their little spiel,
Then I'll go down to the seas again and live
      my life for real.

GERRY HAMILL

'P' MEANS RELIEF IS PERMITTED

Yet another competition requiring unhelpful advice for foreign tourists

Many shops and garages give away free postage stamps.

Prices quoted by taxi drivers, bus conductors and railway booking clerks are open to friendly haggling (you should need to pay about half the original quoted price).

Underground ticket machines take most foreign coins.

PAT BLACKFORD

As in Moscow foreign tourists have preference in London. Always proceed to the head of any queue, merely waving your passport.

P. W. R. FOOT

In Scotland, Gentlemen's Lavatories are indicated by a picture of a man in a kilt.

A. C. C. BRODIE

The Monument commemorates the Great Fire of London: on reaching the top, your party is invited to take part in symbolic firefighting by urinating through the railings onto the heads of the busy fish porters below, who wear bowler hats for protection; they will respond with cheerful waves and merry shouts in their colourful language.

JIM ANTHONY

London barbers are delighted to shave patrons' armpits.

V. F. CORLEONE

You will already doubtless be aware that the Beefeaters at the Tower are unpaid and, like the ducks in St James's Park, rely for provisions on donations from generous passers-by. However, whereas mere 'rankers' may safely be offered ordinary *stewing steak*, only the choicest *rump* or *fillet* should be offered to the Lord Warden of the Tower.

RUFUS STONE

And Stanley J. Sharpless looked ahead to Jubilee Year:

For the Chinese this is the Year of the Snake; for the British it is the Year of the Mug. The Queen's Jubilee is celebrated by the free distribution to all Her Majesty's loyal subjects of:

(1) Portraits showing the Royal mugs.
(2) Mugs showing the Royal portraits.

The latter can be obtained by overseas visitors provided they follow the simple but necessary ritual involved. The procedure is as follows. You go up to any assistant in a shop where these handsome souvenirs are on display and, looking him or her straight in the eye, pronounce these words slowly and clearly,

Jiggity juggernaut
Corgi and pug,
Biggity buggernaut,
I claim this mug.

The assistant will then smile and hand over the mug with a low bow. No payment is made or expected. After bowing in return you run into the street exclaiming, 'I've been mugged! I've been mugged!' whereupon all the passers-by will raise a shout to celebrate your good fortune.

STANLEY J. SHARPLESS

Parking regulations in Britain are simple and logical. The absence of a yellow line by the curb indicates that you may never park there; a broken yellow line, that you may park for part of the day; a solid yellow line, that you may park indefinitely; and a double yellow line, that double parking for extended periods is allowed.

Comments from the public are always welcome in courts of law. When you start speaking an usher will call 'Silence in court' to ensure that you are heard without interruption.

When travelling by train, remember that it is considered impolite not to help anyone who is doing *The Times* crossword puzzle.

PETER ALEXANDER

All the London restaurants listed in this year's editions of the leading gourmet guides have a special offer this summer: half-price meals to parties of *thirty or more* foreign tourists arriving between 7.30 and 9 p.m., Saturday evenings only. Please have passports ready – and, please, to preserve the informality of the occasion, absolutely *no* booking.

Most foreign tourists know that in London they are encouraged to take a piece of fruit, free of charge, from any open-air stall or display.

MICHAEL LIPTON

Bus conductors like to be paid in £5 and £10 notes as they hate carrying heavy coins up and down the stairs.

C. VITA-FINZI

RHYMES OF THE TIMES

Poems for improbable journals

Dltns Wkly

All I wnt is a rm smwhre,
Bdst, flt or pd à trre,
Nce kitch. and bath – wll shre –
As lng as it's nt slvnly;
Frqunt trns – clse to shps and schls,
Bngo, pbs and swmmng pls;
No rnt, no rtes, no rles –
Oh wldn't it be lvvrly.
Oh so lvv-erly lvng abso-blmng-ltly free,
I wld nvr bdge tll bai-lffs cme and evctd me!

All I wnt is a plce to squt,
Tht's nt askng an awfl lt;
So lndlrds wht you gt?
And why are you so lvvrly?
Lvvrly, Lvvrly.

TIM HOPKINS

The Book Collector

A catalogue worth glancing through
Is Susan Spankie's Number Two,
Based on that archetypal hoard,
The Curiosa of a Lord

I noticed there a nice *Justine*,
A trifle foxed, but binding clean,
In tanned contemporary hide
With doublures of she skin inside.

It's just the sort of thing that I,
If I had cash enough, would buy:
It is a tempting thing to see
Binding and content that agree.

PETER PETERSON

Farmers Weekly

How hard the farmer's life is!
If it isn't dry it rains.
The aphis always rife is.
The back-ache always pains.

The thistle always pierces.
The nettle ever stings.
The great bull strong and fierce is.
Each year some murrain brings.

And then townees too clever
To plough, sneer, 'Feather bed!'
When we all know we'll never
Be in that till we're dead.

G. J. BLUNDELL

Exchange and Mart

Music-tackle for band-buffs, and shackles and
    handcuffs and oodles of plastic exotica;
And rubber chair-webbing and works by Krafft-
    Ebing (though comics sell more than erotica);
You can buy C-Thru knickers or PVC stickers
    or rare postage stamps from Rumania,
Or a rare Finnish Spitz or a gleaming Wurlitzer
    (though we cater for whims even zanier);
Spiralled tusks from the narwhal might
    embellish the bar-wall of a pub in Polperro
        or Porlock;
Want bull's pizzles? Or tentacles? Aura
    goggles or pentacles? – a *must* for the leisure-
        time warlock;
Racks for wine or for stretching, a cheap
    Dali etching, architectural drawings
        by Gropius –
Don't look vaguely around, for they're all to
    be found, and lots more, in this mag
    cornucopious.

TOM DONNELLY

GOOD FOR THE SOUL

Confessions of a Book Reviewer, **or other equally rare outpourings**

Woke early, but lay bedbound in a tingling ecstasy of expectation wondering whether a new book parcel from the *Catholic Clarion* could yet have arrived. Rose at Terce to find it had! 798 pages on *Whither Chastity*? Obviously a spiffing good read – if one could ever get round to it. As it was, spent rest of morning sniffing intoxicatingly aromatic glue with which parcel string impregnated and getting higher than Hinsley as a result. Also quite a buzz from delicious book-paper odour. Why is it most books smell better than they read? Passed afternoon in trancedly psychedelic indecision as to precise point at which to penetrate volume's virginity for sample para. Eventually banged it at Page 666 and read fully eight lines. Then spent all of five minutes dictating 900-word review for Miss Maculate to type up in morning. Retired utterly exhausted at Vespers with crate of communion wine. *Q*: Can I possibly survive this insane pace and stress?

ROBIN RAVENSBOURNE

One thing about knocking out these Confessions books, it certainly helps you pull the birds. An ad in the local paper – 'Artist seeks uplifting model' – and you're like a pig in clover. 'Hullo, I'm Denise.' 'Of course you are, dear,' I say, 'now over by the fruit and veg and get 'em off. I want to immortalize you in warm print.' 'Cheeky!' 'No, just the ordinary pose, love.' I sit at my typewriter. *She had charleys as smooth as aubergines surmounted by nipples like loganberries grown under glass.* Well, with the drought this year, things have been getting a bit strained. 'And what do you think of this?' I ask, flashing her the pork chopper. 'Ooooh, it's like . . . a gate-post!' 'That'll do. Over here now.' We fuse into one another. She is as tight as a well-drawn contract. 'What's it like?' I ask, reaching for my notebook. 'Knocks spots off John Braine,' she quips.

PADDY BEESLEY

'Shall I show you my Queen's Opening again?' She giggled. I was exhausted. The worst of reporting these international tournaments, I thought, is the groupies. There are simply far too many of them, wanting to take a plaster cast of your rook. Fischky, the Grand Master, was making love to 23 of them simultaneously, blindfolded of course, but there were still too many. She rolled over, the pattern on her bottom revealing the location of the stalemate problem I had set up hours ago and then unaccountably lost. 'That's the game I've been looking for!' 'As the queen said to the bishop,' she cackled.

MORAY McGOWAN

. . . Shy Sally from Uttoxeter, no longer a maiden after my tip came up for her at Doncaster. I had followed her for weeks, and was finally rewarded. She started slowly, then stretched out, tail threshing, and came like a thunderbolt, finishing a good length up, and could have carried on indefinitely under the weight. I got in at 5 to 1. She finished at 5 to 2. Another filly in my notebook was French Jessie, who took on all comers as a novice, earning a sizeable sum with her places. She liked the flat, but get her over hurdles with the sun on her back, and mademoiselle was game for anything; Most bookies were laying her at Cheltenham. Newcomer Ascot Connie cost me plenty, but I had a feeling this goodlooker would come good. I was on her at a Bath meeting, when she duly obliged. What a jumper! Ah well! Back to racing . . .

PERRY HAMILTON

DIRTY SHEETS

A report on a monarch of yesteryear in the style of our contemporary gutter-press hacks

LUSTY MONARCH'S YAH-BOO TO POPE: 'HENRY RULES, O.K.?'

As every telly-viewer knows, not content with one or two . . . or three or four or five . . . Henry the Eighth had to have sex (oops, sorry!) *six* wives. And when he wasn't bedding 'em he was beheading 'em. When the Pope said he couldn't divorce Catherine of Aragon our maestro of matrimony told him where he could put his Papal Bull, and that's how England became Protestant – Protestant sex led to Protestant sects. Funny thing, history.

(Next week in our grand new series, A Land Fit For Eros To Live In: BALMORAL – or was it? Victoria's Highland Fun and Games. Why was the Queen's favourite song John Brown's Body? Don't miss these startling revelations.)

S. J. KILMINGTON

1977

FOR FREE

Roy Fuller wrote a poem about collecting his free bus pass. Other examples of this genre were asked for.

Betjeman at the Post Office

Fridays, when I draw my pension,
Thoughts I hardly dare to mention
Deep inside of me uncoil;
Through the grille I gaze so sweetly
At Miss Fanshawe, who – how neatly! –
Rubber-stamps my counterfoil.

Brisk the business, bright the glancing,
Slow the lengthy queue advancing
In our High Street GPO;
No room here for doubt or failure,
'What's the airmail to Australia?'
Trust my blue-eyed girl to know.

Senior citizen I may be
But my Civil Service baby
Telescopes the years between;
As she hands the money to me
Half-forgotten lust runs through me –
Senex becomes seventeen.

STANLEY J. SHARPLESS

Dear Sirs, Will you kindly cancel them specs I'm after waitin fifteen years for? Listen till I explain. I wanted to write novels like Elinor Glyn but me eyesight failed, so I ordered bifocals on the National Health and started writin while I waited. I couldn't see worth a damn and got me spellin all wrong and put in a lot of daft lookin words. Every time I looked away I lost me place so I got me syntax wrong. I finished me novel at last and it was a scandal, with the fools of critics sayin I'd a new style on me and it sellin, begob. So I'm not after complainin and I'm stayin as I am, so you can keep your bifocals or give them to some fella that hasn't had my luck. I dictated this letter to Nora, in case you're wonderin. Yours truly, J. Joyce.

PETER ALEXANDER

Your petitioner is the sole survivor from a scheduled disaster area. During the course of the recent catastrophic volcanic activities in the Jordanian Lowlands all my properties and possessions were destroyed: no part of their value is recoverable from my Insurance Company, as the unfortunate occurrences I refer to have been officially declared an Act of God. Under these circumstances I feel that I am not only entitled to full Supplementary Benefit, but also to Legal Aid, which latter is required in order to initiate divorce proceedings against my wife, on the grounds of irretrievable breakdown of our marriage. Never a forward-looking person, she is now completely immobilized, and incapable of performing her marital duties. After all, what can a man do to a pillar of salt? It's enough to make one wish Sodom back again.

PETER PETERSON

PARTY LINES

There is a *Penguin Book of Socialist Verse,* **but no
comparable anthologies for those of different
persuasions. Competitors made good the gap.**

I've taken my gold where I've found it, for
    that's what free enterprise means,
But as for the needy and homeless, I don't
    care a damn row of beans.
I've both of my lads down for Eton, and
    a bloody great Rolls at the door,
So why should I care for the starving?
    It's their fault for being so poor.

We spend lots of tax on their welfare,
    which makes one so very annoyed:
As I often say down at the golf-club,
    it's the lazy who get unemployed.
There's too much taken in taxes, a lesson
    these Reds never learn,
Though I've this useful accountant,
    so I can still spend all I earn.

I'd tell them to pull out their fingers,
    that maxim the Duke likes to give,
But I wouldn't abolish their dole cash,
    for even the poor have to live.
They waste all the pay the state gives 'em
    on sinning and gambling and drink
At my betting shops, pubs, clubs and brothels,
    which is rather a laugh, don't you think?

WAYNE SIDESADDLE

Sideways, lovely liberals,
Sidling up to power,
With old angry Cyril
Grumbling as before.
Steel our Youthful Master
Lead us as we go
Sideways into battle,
Loyal band in tow.
Sideways, then, ye liberals,
Join the Labour throng:
We are not divided,
Power cannot be wrong –
Sideways, lovely liberals
(Never mind the pong).

T. CHEVALLIER

I am a racist of the National Front
And a right good racist too!
I was never very smart
And I couldn't give a fart,
For the blacks – or the Reds like you!
Bad language or abuse I never never use –
Unless it's on the BBC:
'Hey nigger!' I may shout –
If there's only one about,
But I never send him turds or pee.
'What never?'
'No never!'
'What never?'
'Well, *hardly* ever . . .'

TIM HOPKINS

BEASTLY HABITS

The common cormorant, or shag, lays eggs inside a paper bag. Other living things were featured.

The kangaroo's a tidy creature
Because she has a special feature –
I mean the pouch attached in front
To house the new-born kangarunt;
In this she always puts her trash
Like beer-cans, nutshells, cigar ash.
That's why the young when dropped on top
So very quickly learn to hop.

PETER ALEXANDER

'Go to the ant, thou sluggard;
Consider her ways, and be wise.'
Well, I've been to the ant, and I'm buggered
If I think it's one up on us guys;
All that rushing about is damn silly,
(And uneconomic, I bet),
I'd rather consider the lily,
It's got Solomon beat – and *no* sweat.

STANLEY J. SHARPLESS

A young giraffe, when bent on sex,
May find that there are certain checks
When aiming for his partner's bum
And lose his equilibrium;
Not even the keen fire brigade
Can get the creature quite unsplayed.
It really should be better-known
That copulation's safer prone.

M. K. CHEESEMAN

The E-O Parrott weekly romps
Through all the literary comps;
His pile of prizes is so large
That he can own a private barge.
In hopes of blinding readers' eyes
With dust, he goes in for disguise;
But we have found it never hard
To see through Maud and Everard.

JOYCE JOHNSON

FINDE WORDES OLDE

Chaucerian versions of well-known modern English poems

Burialle of the Dede

Aprillé is of al the months moste dyr,
For she engendereth anewe desyr
For fickel fowelés not worthe the winnynge –
And eek the pregnant shayme of former
                    sinnynge.
Aprillé too sends shourés pissynge doune
On them that gathere lilacks all too soune;
And sokes from hed to foote the clevere Dicke
That doth too soune assaie to pick-a-nick.
For Winter, tho' with snowe the waies
                    a'clogging,
Is sesoun meete for boosynge and a'snogging:
Righte dolte be he that doth forbear contry-
                    vinge
In two-faced Janus' hour a deele of swyvinge . . .

MARTIN FAGG

The Summonee's Tale

A MAYDE ther was, y-clept Joan Hunter Dunn,
In all of Surrie, comelier wench was none,
Yet wondrous greet of strength was she with-
                    alle,
Ful lustily she smote the tenis-balle,
And whether lord or lady she wolde pleye,
With thirtie, fortie-love wolde winne the day.
A SQUYER eke ther was, in horseless cariage,
And he wolde fayn have sought her hand in
                    marriage,
Though he coude songes make, with mery rime,
At tennis she out-pleyed him every time;
To make her wyfe he saw but little chaunce,
But then be-thought to take her to a daunce
In gentil Camberlee, where after dark
They held long daliaunce in the cariage park;
Eftsoons Cupide had the twain in thralle,
And this they found the beste game of alle.

STANLEY J. SHARPLESS

AUTO-SUGGESTION

'Would you buy a second-hand car from this man?' Competitors imagined the famous on the forecourt.

IDI AMIN

I'm telling you, dis car for you, man. You buy dis car, you keep out ob trouble. Low mileage. One owner. On dat last I gib you my personal guarantee. Dem little round dents? Dey don't mean nudding, man. Shows she's bullet proof, dat's all. Lick ob paint's all she need. Fine safe car, dis. Dat's right; rattle dem security locks much as you please. Into dis car nobody gets without he knows de combinations. No one going to sneak into dis car slice your balls off. Oh, hullo dere, Sergeant M'Fuzu. Looks to me you got a nice sharp *panga* in your belt dere. Let's hab a feel of it. Boy! Like I thought, sharp like a razor. Howzat? Figure you'll take her? For cash? Dat's great, man, just great. Hand ober der down payment to de Finance Minister. De rest's mine.

Peter Peterson

Mrs WHITEHOUSE

A spotless car, sir. The body clean and pure inside and out. No filth. One gets enough filth on television and radio. Nothing but filth, FILTH! FILTH! . . . oh . . . er . . . excuse me . . . where was I? Ah yes. Gear lever? Hidden under the steering wheel. Young people shouldn't be exposed to that suggestive shaft sticking up their legs, with the digusting knob at the end. This is a *family* car. Show you the room in the back? Look here! Are you suggesting . . . Oh! Sorry! . . . the back *seat* . . . well, quite adequate for unmarried folk choosing to indulge in mixed motoring. Note the coooooool seats. Keeping one's seat cool's *most* important, isn't it? Yes, the interior light's permanently on. As a Christian I like to know what's happening between passengers, don't you? Square dashboard dials? Obviously, Who wants to see two great round things flashing away . . .

Gerry Hamill

OUT AND ABOUT

Sumo wrestling is 'the survival of the fattest'. Definitions of other sports and games were given.

Whippet racing: the curs of the working classes
Fencing: the art of missing the point
Strip poker: the game's not worth the scandal
Professional tennis: gross net profits

BOB SCOTT

Golf: a pitch 'n' sink drama

MORAY McGOWAN

Rambling: the course of the walking class
Bridge: making the best of a bid job

FRANK ANDERSON

Weight-lifting: careless rupture
Golf: taking steps to putt things right

W. H. YOUNG

Shot put: steroids shoving spheroids

JONATHAN FERNSIDE

Sand yachting: keels on wheels
Curling: rolling stones on ice

KEVIN MORRIS

Boxing: the sport of dukes
Drag-racing: the sport of queens

JOHN BENNETT

Stock car racing: bangers and smash

JAMES DOWELL

Transocean ballooning: passing water with a full bladder

GERRY HAMILL

Coursing: splitting hares

JIM ANTHONY

Billiards: pot-luck
Cross channel swimming: might and main
Packer cricket: playing to the salary

V. R. ORMEROD

Pigeon racing: pie in the sky
Backgammon: double, double, you're in trouble

J. TIMSON

Scrabble: crosswords for the clueless

HERODOTUS Q. PLUGHOLE

Karate: chops with everything

PASCOE POLGLAZE

Table tennis: the sport of pings

A. KIDD

Table tennis: where East beats West
Ice hockey: Puck but no fairies

JOHN STANLEY

BEASTLY BAD TASTE

Competitors were requested, and not in vain, to go against the grain and write reactionary poems about the joys of being really rich, nasty, chauvinist, snobbish, racist, etc.

It's all go to Claridges, it's all go the champers,
The Glyndebourne music's such a drag, but
there's always the Fortnum hampers;
We've a town and a country place, of course,
where we keep our gees and doggies,
And we often weekend on the Continent
in spite of the Krauts and Froggies.

Enoch Powell has got it right: deport the
nigs and Pakkis,
The TUC's a bunch of Trots, and their
leaders Moscow lackeys.
We'd give no dole to the unemployed, if
they won't work they're lazy,
We've lots of City directorships, but of what
we're rather hazy.

It's all go to hunt with the Quorn, it's all
go to Ascot,
We've a brand-new Rolls we got as a perk,
with our family crest as a mascot.
The Socialists tax us too much, we've always
voted Tory,
But we'll not say how we made our pile,
for that's another story.

E. O. PARROTT

202

I'd shoot all commies out of hand and set
                              the people free,
For no right-winger in the land is more
                              right-wing than me.
Each member of the National Front's
                    a long-haired left-wing pouf,
And Vorster's latest liberal stunt is bloody
                              marxist stuff.

I'd birch and lash and flay and flog
                    those author chaps obscene,
And castrate every bloody wog to keep
                         our culture clean.
I'd have all labour unions banned, I'd jail
                              the TUC,
For no right-winger in the land is more
                              right-wing than me.

A private army I'd recruit of decent,
                         loyal chaps,
I'd train them to put in the boot wherever
                         there's a lapse
From due respect, which I demand, for
                         each minority,
For no right-winger in the land is more
                              right-wing than me.

GERRY HAMILL

I grab and grudge and itch and leer
And strut and swagger and scorn and sneer
And drool and bite and suck and screw
And gobble and gorge and swill and spew
And lounge and laze and loaf and slouch
And rage and kick and splutter and grouch
And *I* don't need your analyst's couch.

TOM DONNELLY

I'm stinkingly rich and I love it,
I'm loaded with perks and with pelf.
If you've got a 'good cause' you can shove it;
I'm keeping the lot for myself.

Let the niggers go back where they came from
(Though as servants they're useful and cheap).
Still, I'll give them a wave, all the same, from
My place at the top of the heap.

I've a yacht where my jet-setting friends meet,
Four houses, a beautiful Rolls.
Let the poor scrimp and save to make
                              ends meet;
Let *their* pips, not mine, squeak, poor souls!

M. GOODRICH

BY-LINES

Go tell our master,
All you passers-by,
That here, obedient to his laws,
We lie.

Thus runs an epitaph for journalists. Similar efforts were
required for other professions.

A Modern Theologian

In learned language he opined
That Christ was just a bloke;
God grinned, while promptly adding him
To Hell's supply of coke.

A Reviewer

In death she pays the penalty
For reams of gush and gabble;
Condemned to read, through endless time,
The *oeuvre* of Margaret Drabble.

A Schoolmaster

Dead and burnt and scattered now,
No wisp of him survives,
Save half-remembered thoughts and whims
Built into others' lives

A Police Officer

This little pig worked in Soho;
This little pig took his cut;
This little pig was grassed on;
This little pig's gone phut.

MARTIN FAGG

Dons

Death caught us unawares
(We *must* do something about those stairs).

V. F. CORLEONE

A Composer

I've lived a life of flats and sharps,
Adapting and transposing;
Don't think I'm working now on harps,
I'm simply *de*composing.

A Popular Novelist

Grieve not, dear reader, though
This be my final plot,
For I am still below
Producing further rot.

JOYCE JOHNSON

A Politician

I never retired; I died in
My boots;
Even now I'm consulting the
Grass roots.

T. CHEVALLIER

A Builder

My estimate was such & such:
This stone alone cost twice as much

FOXIE

UNAUTHORISED VERSIONS

Passages from the Bible recast in the style of any humorous writer

'Holy smoke Jeeves!' I exclaimed, as the last of the Baal bimboes gave up the fire-lighting effort. 'That looks pretty grim, what!'

'It must be admitted, sir,' said Jeeves, 'that circumstances could be more propitious.'

'Holy smoke is precisely what poor old Elijah is going to need. Do we pray, Jeeves?'

'It will not be necessary, sir,' said Jeeves, calmly. 'If you will observe, Mr Elijah has already succeeded in igniting his bonfire.'

And, dash it all, you know, so he had!

'Jeeves!' I said, 'I believe you had something to do with this!'

'Well, sir,' the blighter replied, 'I did take the liberty of surreptitiously inserting some paraffin-soaked rags into Mr Elijah's bonfire.'

'But the rags – ?'

'You will doubtless recall the purple-striped robe you recently purchased for evening wear, sir? I am afraid I was obliged to use that. It really did not become you, sir.'

G. J. BLUNDELL

After their first rash sex
Adam and Eve wore a *cache-sexe*;
He said, 'This stunt'll
Avoid the embarrassment of a full frontal.
(Good thing fig leaves
Are big leaves).'

STANLEY J. SHARPLESS

Which just shows how dumb it was of God to
strike *Apfelstrudel*
Off the paradisal Bill of Fare, because if there's
one food all Women have a yen for
It's the one item that *isn't* on the menu (and
what are men for
Except to get it for them?) – but whereas
Adam merely thought it *droll*
That the Biggest Daddy of Them All had
banned the one food that all reliable dietary
experts agree is utterly bereft of cholesterol,
Our Great-Grand-Mammy
(Who hailed from the Deep South of Adam's
rib-cage – the anatomical equivalent
of Alabammy)
Said: 'Ah don't think it's funny,
Honey,
When a lady has to beg pardon
For pluckin' the fruit of her *own* Garden –
And this gentleman-caller who came this
mornin' – and I do declare that ah've never
yet met a sobra
Cobra . . .'

SIMON LITTIMER

There was an Old Man with a beard,
Who said, 'I demand to be feared!
Address me as God,
And love me, you sod!'
And Man did just that, which is weird.

NAOMI MARKS

205

WUTHERING DEPTHS

Gone With The Wind **has spawned** *Tara*. **Blurbs were required for a sequel to any classic.**

Twenty years after their appearance in *Lord of the Flies* the boys, now in their thirties, reunite for the first time in a hotel on the Isle of Wight. In *Return of the Castaways* we again meet Piggy, a balding, overweight, highly successful businessman trading in ladies under-garments from his giant warehouse in Camberley; Jack, manic-depressive homosexual, pig farmer and boy scout leader; Ralph, author of an unsuccessful book on survival technique, accompanied by his beautiful wife Laura (providing a welcome female interest the earlier book lacked) who is still waiting for her 15 year old marriage to be consummated. What happens in the final devastating chapter, when a sex-crazed Jack and Laura make a play for Piggy in the hotel's Hawaiian bar, makes the incidents in *Lord of the Flies* seem like a cosy garden tea party in comparison.

DOUGLAS ITTO

If you read Alexander Solzhenitsyn's brilliant masterpiece *A Day in the Life of Ivan Denisovich* you'll want to read the astounding follow-up *Another Day in the Life of Ivan Denisovich*. This excitingly original novel – written following Solzhenitsyn's flight to the West and first serialised in the *Daily Mail* – is intended to form the second volume of Solzhenitsyn's trilogy *Three Days in the Life of Ivan Denisovich*; it follows Ivan Denisovich Shukhov as he smuggles another piece of hacksaw blade into the prison camp, steals another bowl of porridge, builds a wall and denounces the pacifist policies of detente practised by the West. Now, for the first time, Solzhenitsyn dares to reveal the secrets of life in one of the special labour camps manufacturing spare parts for NATO tanks. This startling and sometimes shocking novel is one that you won't want to escape from!

JONATHAN M. BATES

Lolita was a *succès fou*, a *succès de scandale*, an outrageous success by any reckoning. Here is its dazzling sequel: *Forever Lolita*. In this (alas) posthumously published novel Nabokov brings Humbert Humbert and his eponymous nymphet together again. It relates how the famous (or some would say, infamous) pair take off from Cape Kennedy on a tour of the universe in a rocket designed to travel at the speed of light. At this speed, the author explains, time stands still for space travellers, so Humbert achieves his ultimate ambition of enjoying his nymphet for all eternity, secure in the knowledge that she will never age by so much as a single day. Nabokov soars to new heights of imaginative realism in this happy blend of Science Fiction and Sex – a veritable *tour de force* of inter-galactic paedophilia.

'A space probe with a difference' (*Astronauts Weekly*).

STANLEY J. SHARPLESS

A HANDFUL OF BUST

If Conrad rewrote Henry James the result might be *The Turn of the Crew.*
So what else is new?

Connolly/Molly Parkin: *Enemas of Promise*

PADDY BEESLEY

Osborne/Betjeman: *Look Back in Ongar*
Orwell/Dick Francis: *Animal Form*

E. M. O. ELSE and D. M. FIELD

James/Conrad: *The Astern Papers*
Izaac Walton/H. Wilson: *The Compleat Wangler*

JOHN BENNETT

L. Lee/Wilde: *Cider with Bosie*

F. M. TOLLEY

Lawrence/Richard Gordon:
Lady Chatterley's Liver
Flaubert/Henry Miller: *Madame Ovary*

R. D. CONDON

I. Amin/Anna Sewell: *Black Booty*
E. Waugh/P. Hain: *Vile Bobbies*

W. S. BROWNLIE

Anthony Burgess/Desmond Morris:
A Clockwork Orang

MICHAEL BIRT

E. Waugh/Health Education Council:
Put Out More Fags
Macdonald Fraser/De Sade: *Lashman*

TOM DONNELLY

Hemingway/Trollope: *The Old Men and the See*

W. H. YOUNG

Wilde/Elizabeth David: *Lady Windermere's Flan*

MARY SCOTT

Tom Stoppard/Trotsky: *Dirty Lenin*

RUSSELL LUCAS

Dante/Noël Coward: *The Too-Divine Comedy*

TIM O'DOWDA

Kipling/Richard Ingrams: *Just-Sue Stories*

COLIN PHILLIPS

Wilkie Collins/Germaine Greer:
Woman in White's

JIM ANTHONY

Proust/Martin Fagg:
A la Recherche du Comps Perdu

PETER ALEXANDER

POSITIONS VACANT

Advertisements for brides, in verse

Come live with me and be my M/S
And earn a princely bonus, *viz*:
The charm of my society,
Whose scintillant variety
Will momently reveal why I
Am just the sort of modest guy
Who (serious but *never* solemn)
Employs the STATESMAN's 'Personal Column'
To itemise his giant ego
(Constructed out of psychic Lego);
Then sits and broods and wonders why
No dolly ever *dare* reply . . .

MARTIN FAGG

A young ex-beauty queen required,
By Salt Lake City ex-church-head,
Change of employment now desired,
Willing to supply own chains and bed.

WAYNE SIDESADDLE

It's no go the Hite Report, it's no go the
Libbers,
All I want is a nubile wench to fetch my
carpet slippers.

Computer dating sounded fine, I gave 'em all
the info,
Got fixed up with a one-armed schizoid
Serbo-Croat nympho;
Did my damnedest in the circs to play the
perfect lover,
Found out pretty soon there wasn't any need
to bother.

It's no go the fat ones, it's no go the lean,
All I want is sympathy and a trip down
mammary lane.

It's no go your feelthy pix, it's no go Lolita,
It's no go the pantie adverts on the escalator,
It's no go the French lessons, it's no go
the saunas,
All I want is a female friend who's ready to
cut corners.

STANLEY J. SHARPLESS

ROCK BOTTOM

Punk versions of any traditional ditty

Some talk of Punks like Georgie Git, Vic
    Vomit, Les Latrine;
Of Groups like 'Crabs' and 'Supershit', 'The
    Dildoes', 'Clap', 'Yobscene'.
But of all your foul and filthy freaks there's
    none that can compare
With the wham-bam-slam-bam-scram-mam
    Splat! of us lads in 'Pubic Hair'.

We've raped five nuns, three peeresses and one
    expectant mother;
And on the road between the gigs we gaily
    screw each other.
For of all your penile pistoleers there's none
    that can compare
With the quick-flick-slick-dick-lick-dick Splut!
    of us ginks in 'Pubic Hair'.

We tint our thatch a tasteful puce – or else
    bright tangerine;
With acid in our orange juice we can act sod-
    ding mean.
And when it comes to 'bottling' Fuzz there's
    none that can compare
With the crash-bash-clash-lash-smash-gash
    Sploing! of us guys in 'Pubic Hair'.

TERRY TOWLING

There's a mortuary next door,
Nelly Dean,
Where they'll shove you in a drawer,
Nelly Dean;
When I've ate your brains for starters,
And I've used your guts for garters,
I'll be red in tooth and claw,
Nelly Dean.

There'll be lots of lovely gore,
Nelly Dean,
When they scrape you off the floor,
Nelly Dean,
Of all the draggy brasses,
With slack and saggy arses,
You're the one I most abhor,
Nelly Dean.

RODDY REDDING

SHINING LIGHTS

With an eye on Kingsley Amis's *Oxford Book of Light Verse,*
competitors wrote on any modern topic in the style of a light-verse master

The Victor Vanquished: A Tall Story
(after Thomas Hood)

Young Victor's zoo-mate greeted him
With high-pitched girlish laughter,
'You've got a neck,' she slyly said,
'If necking's what giraffeter.'

'You've guessed aright,' Victor replied,
Not slow to take his cue,
'Come – be my mate – I'll demonstrate
I can knock spots off you.'

Thus saying, Victor mounted her
And started amorous play,
Which turned quite unexpectedly
To a bizarre dis-splay.

He did the splits but failed to rise,
Although he strained and kicked – oh
What a lovely way to die,
In flagrante delicto.

STANLEY J. SHARPLESS

The More, the Meedier
(after Ogden Nash)

Things in Britain seem to be getting seedier
                                    and seedier:
Or is it just the meedier?
Sometimes I ask myself why it is that meedier
                        men almost never choose
To lay off the bad news.
I mean, look at the way they go on
                                about Grunwick,
A subject you'd think everybody would be only
                        too happy to have done wick.
And then there's Jeremy:
I admit the poor guy is his own worst enemy,
But is that any reason why meedier men should
                                    yell and yodel
The whole goddam time about that
                                    male model?
And why do they keep showing us the fuzzy
            face of a young prig who took his tape
                        recorder into a banquet,
Expecting to be thanket?
Personally, I suggest they put on a new record,
    and start telling us how wonderful things are
                            in Britain for a change:
Or else go catch mange.

PETER PETERSON

210

WELL CAUGHT

Slogans and adages which might become popular in time and get themselves included in the second edition of Eric Partridge's *Dictionary of Catch Phrases*

Wiping the slater clean: an impossibly difficult task; cf. *cleaning the Augean Stables.*

All clean-up and whitehouse fashion: no 'bristols'.

It works like a leyland: it doesn't work at all; or, more colloq., it came to pieces in my hand.

MAUD GRACECHURCH

As nutty as a lordell: as mad or impracticable as possible. (Originally *As nutty as Lord L,* referring to the familiar abbreviation for an eccentric peer, apparently notorious during his lifetime, now forgotten.)

E. O. PARROTT

Jay's fluid: clever P.R.; applied esp. to one who is facile, quick, with astringent manner yet calming phraseology; high class 'flannel'.

Wearing my Jack Jones: going through a phase of self-imposed austerity; being ostentatiously monkish. (Jack Jones was a prominent Trade Union leader famous for his puritanism. A *Jack Jones* came to mean both a cloth cap and a hair shirt.)

T. GRIFFITHS

It's in the mailbag: converse of *It's in the bag,* a warning that some projected undertaking is likely to be difficult, expensive, delayed, hazardous or perhaps simply impossible.

I've sold it to Reggie: implies that the speaker has conducted a transaction which materially benefits the other party on the implicit promise of future unspecified rewards.

BASIL RANSOME

To benn the cabinet: to frustrate action by incessant talk.

To do a Harold: to give an honour which is worth nothing, or which works in a negative fashion.

M. K. CHEESEMAN

BR: BEECHING'S REMAINS

The names of many large organisations are really acronyms. Competitors translated them.

PONTINS: Plethora Of Noisy Trippers In Nasty Shacks.

ALITALIA: Aircraft Landing In Tokyo. All Luggage In Amsterdam.

SABENA: Such A Bloody Experience. Never Again.

JOHN STANLEY

ALITALIA: Always Late In Take-off, Always Late In Arriving.

TWA: Try Walking Across.

PAUL PASTOR

WOOLWORTHS: We Overwork Old Ladies, Wickedly Overcharge, & Rule The High Street.

LAMBETH COUNCIL: London's Amorphous Mass of Badly Educated Twits, Hacks, Chronically Overpaid Underworked Nearly Certifiable Idiots & Layabouts.

J. Y. WATSON

PLAYERS: Percolates Lungs And Your Entire Respiratory System.

ROGER DUNKLEY

HARRODS: Have A Rolls Royce On Daddy, Sweetie.

GUINNESS: Gasus! Doant Oirishmen No A Foine Thrink Wan Dey Get Ut??

GERRY HAMILL

LONDON RUBBER CO: Little Ones Naturally Disposed Of; Normal Relationships Uninterrupted; But, Bratlessness Entails Rolling Carefully Off!

JETHRO B. TUCKETT

ILEA: Illiterate Louts Explained Away.

A. D. BEROWNE

FISONS: Frightful Insects Spoil Our Nice Salads.

RUSSELL LUCAS

BOOTS: Buy One On The Sly!

PASCOE POLGLAZE

WATNEY: Weaker And Tasting Nastier Every Year.

H. WOODS

NUR: No Use Rushing.

R. BURNS

SOTHEBYS: Selling Off The Heirlooms Enriches Blokes, You See.

JIM ANTHONY

ACCESS: A Credit Card Encourages Silly Spending.

NHS: No Hope of Surgery.

J. TIMSON

W. H. SMITH: Won't Have Smutty Mags In The House.

LAING: Largely Alcoholic Irish Navvy Gangs.

SUE DE NIMM

LLOYDS: Lend Lolly On Your Dodgy Security?

MIDLAND: Millions In Deposits – Loans Are Naturally Denied.

BASIL RANSOME

WALLS: Will Anne Like Loverboy's Sausages?

WIMPY: We Include More Potato Yearly.

PETER RUMNEY

SHAM

Apposite anagrams of the names of TV programmes

The Big Match: Thematic G.B.H.

The Dick Emery Show: The comedy we shirk.

W. J. WEBSTER

The Monday Film: Money-mad filth.

BOB SCOTT

The World of Pam Ayres:
  Flawed or sham poetry.
  Poems? O, few! Art? Hardly!
  O, me, what dreary flops.

K. WYKE

I Claudius: U Suicidal.

J. A. FRANKLIN

Nationwide: Wan edition.

MARCUS BOLT

Bruce Forsyth and the Generation Game:
  See 'B' gyrating Anthea Redfern too much.

FRANK ANDERSON

The Virginian: Virgin he ain't!

The Pam Ayres Show: How me trash PAYES!

ROBERT BAIRD

The Old Grey Whistle Test: Let's wheedle
  grotty hits.

KEVIN MORRIS

Newsday: De yawns.

J. E. MILLER

Bruce Forsyth and the Generation Game:
  Brute force meeting shy dragon Anthea.

JOHN P. SPARROW

Conservative Party Political Broadcast: Or
  does a Tory V.I.P. accept trivia, cant, balls?

ALLAN SCOTT

IF THE NAME FITS

Apposite anagrams of the names of fictional characters

Desdemona: One dead Ms.

JOYCE JOHNSON

Sally Bowles: Yes, blows all.
Humbert Humbert: Rub them, rub them.

SMASHER RANSOME

Moll Flanders: Fallen old Mrs.

W. F. N. WATSON

Miss Moneypenny: Men, yon spy's mine!

G. E. R. MADDEN

Lord Peter Wimsey: Wrily modest peer.

A. R. BLACKSHIELD

Miss Joan Hunter Dunn: Man-rush'd tennis Juno.

E. M. WALKER

Man Friday: Damn fairy!
Alexander Portnoy: Exalted porno yarn.

JEAN PASTOR

Madame Bovary: A very bad moma.

ANTHONY DONEGAN

Lolita: Lo! Tail!

GERRY HAMILL

Moll Flanders: Small fondler.

CHRIS CLARK

Desdemona: De Mean Sod!

TIM HOPKINS

EYEBALLS TO EYEBALLS

After the Frost-Nixon interviews, almost any other encounter seemed possible.

DEREK NIMMO: And now the first and most famous of all Beauty Queens . . . the face that launched a thousand ships . . . fabulous HELEN OF TROY. Lovely to see you, Helen. Tell me, was it really true about all those ships?

HELEN: Well actually, Derek I did launch one, once, but I think my press agent stuck on a few noughts.

D.N.: Oh-oh-oh, I *am* surprised at him. Now let's see – you come from a very distinguished family, don't you?

H.: You can say that again.

D.N.: Your father, Zeus, met your mother, Leda, while swan-upping. You yourself married the famous Menelaus. I guess that was the secret dream of all you young Grecian girls: 'One day the right men'll lay us.' Then you had that affair with Paris. You see, I've done my Homer-work. By the way, I'm sure viewers will want to know how you keep so beautifully slim.

H.: I joined the Troy Weight Watchers.

D.N.: *(to camera)* As witty as she's lovely, isn't she? Now, Helen, tell us about those Topless Towers of Ilium . . .

STANLEY J. SHARPLESS

HARRY CARPENTER: I understand this was something of a needle match?

GOLIATH: Yeah, well, Harry, there was a bit of aggro like, on account of him being a little Israelite prat. Know what I mean?

H.C.: You've been called a dirty fighter in the past; what's your reaction to this?

G.: Well, you'd better ask my manager about that, Harry; I just get in there and slash with me sword.

H.C.: You're not concerned with the artistic aspects of the fight game?

G.: Bloody Philistine 'en't I?

H.C.: And what did you think of the Israelites choosing a smaller man to take you on?

G.: If you ask me, Harry, they were all making bets on the side – crafty buggers!

H.C.: And what do *you* think about David's giving you a couple of stone?

G.: Didn't you see the fight, Harry? He give *me* a stone.

TIM HOPKINS

'...there was a bit of aggro like'

MORE SAINTS

St Thomas More is the only MP ever to be canonised. Claims were put forward on behalf of more recent Members, in the style of Laureates.

WORDSWORTH ON LLOYD GEORGE

I met a little cottage-girl;
She strutted by my side.
'Now tell me, little maid,' asked I,
'Whence comes such sinful pride?'
'Why, Lloyd George knew my father, sir,'
This innocent child replied.
'And father knew Lloyd George,' said she,
'And mother did as well.'
Her childish laughter in my ears
Rang like a silver bell.
He whom a wise child honours thus
Must sure in heaven dwell.

MARY VISICK

CIBBER ON SIR HAROLD

Britannia, hark, the seraphim have caroll'd
The worthy sainthood of thy fair Sir Harold.
His books reveal'd the paragon he's been,
Belov'd of Heav'n and, better still, the Queen.

A man who loved the Right, though socialist,
He rightly steer'd thy ship of state, I wist.
On his motley crew, great honours he bestowed
Ere he forsook his Captaincy's great load.

Wise and yet modest, as his own words do show,
And since he's quick, he's quick to tell thee so.
Though Briton's poor, thy saint is not to blame:
His white hot fire hath left thy land the same.

A. BOTEMAN

TENNYSON ON BENN

He comes from haunts of dukes and dons,
He knocks his *own* Aunt Sally,
A man of Gold among the Bronze –
Patrician in the galley!

His truth is not beset with doubt,
He sees no Leyland failing;
And who can blame his boyish pout,
When mortal fools are railing?

His soul's eternal; this I know
(Like Alfred's brimming river).
While Right and Centre change and grow,
The Left goes on for ever!

T. HOPE

1978

DIAL 999

Nonets in which the subject's name must appear in the first line

Zek, a woman of the Sabine tribe,
Said 'I'm upset, as I'll describe.
All these chaps came on this raid,
And did things. I'm afraid
Some girls had real fun,
But I got none.'
'You,' said one,
'Not rape
Shape.'   WAYNE SIDESADDLE

Michelangelo Buonarotti
Thought the Pope distinctly potty
Wanting the Sistine Ceiling
Tutto Fresco. Kneeling
On a sort of sling,
He knocked the thing
Off – and how!
Look now . . .
WOW!   MOLLY FITTON

That realistic author Tolkien
Said 'What do my novels all mean?
I fear those fey elven folk
Are just a bad joke;
Yet Gandalf the Grey
Really does pay.
So don't gripe,
Just type
Tripe.'   M. K. CHEESEMAN

Jacqueline Kennedy Onassis
Had no temps for Tom, and dumped Dick
To marry Ari, who had masses,
Liked classy lasses: sic
Transit Gloria.
The story o-
F her life's: 'Wi-
Dow wi'
Dough.'   WILL BELLENGER

Militant fury, Queen Boudicca,
Fixed scythes to the wheels of her char-
Iot, saying, 'These will cut
Anything that may jut;
They're fine dissuaders
Of invaders.
First-aiders
Can't fix
Pricks.'   HARRISON EVERARD

Hi there! My name is Jimmy Carter,
Once considered a non-starter;
My spectacular progress
Is due to God, I guess.
But what is success?
Peanuts, merely,
Which clearly
Explains
Plains.   STANLEY J. SHARPLESS

Cranmer took King Henry the Eighth's side
And favoured the Royal Divorce,
Thus becoming Arch. of Cant.;
But when the Queen Regnant
was Mary, of course
Cranmer changed hors-
es; was tried,
and died,
fried.   JOYCE JOHNSON

PHIL McCAVITY, DENTIST

Double-barrelled names which enclose the profession of their bearers

Ben Dover-Boyes, the public school master

HAZEL STANLEY

Juno Watts-Cumming, the soothsayer
Anastasia Mostyn-Winter, the regular guest

JOHN STANLEY

Mark Howitt-Burns, the arsonist

STANLEY J. SHARPLESS

Walter Wall-Wilton, the carpet salesman

R. M. LYNN

Livia Gunza-D'Ador, the Mafia receptionist
Harry Chooker-Folland, the Channel ferry
   operator

W. J. WEBSTER

Anna Pollock-Steer-Royde, the woman discus
   champion

W. S. BROWNLIE

Sheila Bligh-Cheeseleigh, the prostitute

R. D. CONDON

Robin ffolkes-Knightley, petty thief

IAN BARNES

Isadora Dora-Knott, the philosopher

JANET ALDIS-PLAYER

Annie Busby-Hinde, the conductress
Digby Lowe-Sandys, the egyptologist

BARRY ANTHONY

Fanny Dunn-Browne, the nudist

CLAUDE SPETTIGUE

Sir Vere de Scomfert-Heald, the surgeon

ERIC McPHERSON

Mordecai Ford-Rilling, the dentist
Ivor Rees-Bangor, the pub pianist

GERRY HAMILL

Hugh Zapretti-Boyden, the budgerigar breeder

MARGARET WEBB

Lettice Makeham-Littler, the masseuse

ALASTAIR CHAMBERS

Gail Wynns-Cumming, the weather forecaster

CARY LUTON-LIGHTFOOT

Ivor Carter-Wynne, the racing driver

ISABEL EMMETT

Hugh Wood-Woodger, the policeman

MYRA RICE

Sheila Paula Mannin-Bedd, the nymphomaniac

LAURENCE FOWLER

Hester Wright-Daly, the journalist

WILLIAM HODSON

Celia Lettuce-Downe, the office despatch clerk

COLIN GARRETT

WITH THE NEW BLUE WHITENER

Advertising copy for any political party

VOICE: We asked Mrs Jill Knight of Edgbaston to part with her TORY principles for a week . . . (*camera turns to Mrs Knight*), So you're prepared to part with your TORY principles for a week, are you, Jill?

JILL: I am, yes.

VOICE: And you're going to try out this other brand for us?

JILL: That's right, Desmond.

VOICE: One week later, we visited Jill again, to see how she'd got on. (*camera turns to Mrs Knight*) How did you get on, Jill?

JILL: Oh, (*grimace*) terrible. My old principles would have shifted these black and brown stains by now; the maid's bleached my 10 per cent guidelines; the kids have been striking for higher pocket money; the dog's been mugged by the postman; and look, will you come and look at this? (*camera follows Jill to bedroom, where she lifts the bed up*) Reds under here – it's shocking, Desmond. My TORY principles would have had them out by now.

VOICE: So you'd like your TORY principles back, would you?

JILL: Absolutely, Desmond.

VOICE: (*with a slight chuckle*) Sure?

JILL: Oh, definitely. (*camera freezes on Mrs Knight*)

VOICE: So there you are. Proof you can trust TORY every time. And that's a Fact.

BILL GREENWELL

CALLER: Good morning Madam. I've called about the smell on the landing.

LANDLADY: Oh, come in, It don't 'alf pen an' ink! Somethin' awful!

CALLER: May I go upstairs and – er – sniff around?

LANDLADY: Certainly. Anythin' to get rid of that 'orrible pong!

CALLER: (*sniffs*) I think I know the trouble. Have you got any *Socialists* living here?

LANDLADY: Well, there's two lodgers. Charlie's a chop suey or somefing up Leylands, 'Arry, 'e's a Works Convenience . . .

CALLER: Kick 'em out!

LANDLADY: Eh?

CALLER: Socialists are musty, mouldy, dingy and wet. They spread dry rot throughout Britain.

LANDLADY: Good 'eavens!

CALLER: *And* IMF's prognostications postulate an ongoing negative economic situation, come 1980!

LANDLADY: Well I never!

CALLER: *And* before you can turn round they'll nationalise your Guest House behind your back!

LANDLADY: Ooer!

CALLER: Put Mrs Thatcher in. She'll . . .

LANDLADY: I don't 'ave women lodgers.

CALLER: . . . make your landing fresh and clean! *Only the Conservatives make nasty smells DISAPPEAR LIKE MAGIC!*

GERRY HAMILL

CONSERVATIVE POWER WILL DO MORE FOR YOU –
Because it's biological

Stubborn, everyday problems are part of life. They come out of our most fundamental urges. The urge to get on in the world. To keep what belongs to us. To give our families the best. To stand on our own two feet. These are all natural human instincts. They're biological. And only the Conservatives really understand them, because only the Conservatives think *biologically*.

Other parties try to wash away problems with man-made theories. They never work. Life is too deep for them. You need a biological power – the power of the Conservatives – to get right down where it matters. And then you'll see things start to shift! If you voted right last time, you won't want to swap now. But if you didn't, why not cross over to the Conservative Party? It's only natural, after all.

W. J. WEBSTER

HENRY IV PART 3

Speeches from Shakespeare's lost history plays

King Canute

*The coast near Southampton. Enter, from royal barge,
Canute, courtiers and Fool.*
Fool: 'Tis clear, Great Dane, thy barque's
                worse than thy bite.
Canute: Once more unto the beach, dear friends,
                once more –
Fool: A line, methinks, too good to throw away,
'Twill soon be echoed in another play.
Canute: – For now I needs must show these
                slavering curs
That e'en Canute cannot roll back the sea.
Fool: Canute cannot? Cannot Canute?
                For shame!
Canute: Cease, fool. We at the mighty ocean's
                marge.
Exchanging throne for deck-chair for the
                nonce,
Shall thus disport, paddling our royal feet.
Fool: Nay, if it please thee, paddle thine
                own, Canute,
And get thy breeches wet into the bargain,
But why not summon statecraft to thine aid
And make a secret compact with the moon?
Sit tight until the tide is on the turn,
Then it would seem as though thy royal
                command,
'Back, waters, back', had wrought a miracle.
Canute: Verily, my boy, thou'rt on the ball.
Fool: On land or sea, good sire, timing is all.
Canute: Henceforth I'll hear no ill spoken of fools.
Fool: Thou rul'st the waves; my task's to
                waive the rules.

Stanley J. Sharpless

King John Part Two

Another part of the sea-shore. Enter the Bishop of Ely and clown.

Clown: Marry, 'tis a very vile piss-pot of a sea that can so affront the King, and thy sea shall rue it.

Ely: My see is all upon dry land, sirrah.

Clown: And that is the sort of sea to have. This sea is as wet as the Great Bed of Ware after the old knight had slept therein. Marry, it means to wash my feet also.

Ely: Indeed it is the Wash. But fear not, for the tide is on the turn.

Clown: Then my feet, not being tired, can run away from his vile Wash that thinks that can wash righter than the King. Hold, see the sea doth not know thy rides, thou naughty bishop, for am I not now the owner of two very wet legs?

Ely: Come, bring me where the King lies.

Clown: Marry, will I though it is thou that lieth about the sea and not the King.

MAUD GRACECHURCH

Richard Coeur-de-Lion

A Castle in Austria: Richard's quarters.

Richard: Let luckless John drudge out the
                care of kings,
While I, high Austria's guest, sequester'd here,
With feast and frolic, dalliance and wine,
Yet longer piece my most protractive stay.
Though not incarcerate, I have it nois'd
Abroad that I am so, lest busy Albion's
Sleek burgesses should chide my duty scanted –
For nothing irks the sluggard English so
As looking on at others' idleness.
All vacancy I'll cram with authorship
And badge myself a very Alexander –
The merest dolts all gen'rals else. To long
Crusades, long cross'd by fate, what meeter end
Than crucifying fellow captain's fame?
A hideous twanging and caterwauling without.
Alack! Doth raucous punk pursue me yet?
He pokes head through aperture.
Thy din belt up, most unmelodious knave –
Of thy rude strings pray leave the plucking off!

Blondel: At last, my sovereign prince,
                my warblings wild
Have found thee out! Fear not, most
                honey lord –
My tidings sped, thou shalt be ransom'd straight.
He hurries off.

Richard: Behold in this the scourge of
                modern days:
Where busybodies bide, thou canst not win.

COLIN KIMBERLEY

MY OLD TOUCH

**Music-hall songs chronicling the joys and sorrows
of modern working-class life**

I was signing on as usual – the day was damp
                  and muggy;
Just signing on as usual – the office air was fuggy;
When there behind the counter, I beheld this
                scrumptious bird;
I felt the prick of Cupid – tho' it wasn't *his*
                that stirred!

Chorus:
    Just signing on as usual –
    When Fate said 'Meet the wife';
    And all at once just signing on
    Meant signing on for life.

Her Allowances are generous, her Increments
                are vast;
Her Supplementary Benefits are
              wholly unsurpassed.
Before I met my Mirabelle, my life was just
                a void –
Now, exploring my Entitlement, I'm
            never unemployed!

TERRY TOWLING

I'm a single-parent Mum 'oo 'as a quiverful
                of kids
Gettin' something supplement'ry from me
              lodger.
Now yer musn't supplement the Welfare's
            supplement'ry quids
Or they'll prosecute yer for a shameless dodger.

Chorus:
So me lodger 'ad to go though I fancied 'im galore
An' I miss 'is supplement'ry that's for sure.
'Ave a nibble an' they quibble 'cos yer *must* be
           chaste an' pure
Before them civil servants make yer socially
           secure.

When the Welfare Lady sez 'Ai heah you
           entertains a gent,
Would 'e be . . . Ah . . . a-having of the other?'
I answer 'Eow! Yer narsty maind! that party
           wot 'as spent
Some time wiv me's me ever-loving brother!
So me lodger 'ad to go *etc.*

GERRY HAMILL

CURE-ALLS

What if Charmian had had some snake-bite serum, or if Anna Karenina had called the Samaritans? Famous scenes rewritten

The Barge She Sat In

Charmian: What hast thou there?
Cleopatra: The certain instrument of my
    undoing (*Undoes bra*)
  Now shalt thou see the serpent of old Nile
  Another serpent to her bosom take;
  A mother once, a mummy soon to be.

    (Applies asp to breast)
Char: What dreadful jest is this?
Cleo: When I am dead, good wench, thou
                    canst explain
  How on this very couch was Cleo lain.
Char: Nay, nay – I have a sov'reign remedy.
Cleo: 'Tis very apt. A sov'reign remedy. Ha!
Char: A simple, madam, highly spoken of,
  Made to an old Egyptian recipe,
  With locusts, bitter herbs and camel dung,
  One guaranteed to cure all mortal ills,
  Snake-bites and boils and other royal
                    distempers,
  Jaundice, pimples, the plague – thou
                    namest it.

    (Applies serum to affected area)
Cleo: 'Tis magic, sure; the sting abates already.
  So shall I live to fight another day,
  And – the gods willing – in another play.

        STANLEY J. SHARPLESS

Mañana

Macbeth: Wherefore was that cry?
Seyton: The queen, my lord, is waked.
Macbeth: You mean she's cured?
Seyton: Indeed, her doctor that observed
                    her sighs,
  Her strange insistence that some spots
                    of blood
  Prevented her from having forty winks,
  Kip that knits up the ravelled sleeve of care,
  This doctor hath sent out to Dunsinane
  To Boots for downers. These administered,
  She slept this fortnight. She's much
                  better now.
Macbeth: She should have died. Hereafter
  There would have been a time for just
                    a word
  From me between her nagging.
                  'Hubby, please,
  Oh, just one murder more.' It never stops.
  Tomorrow, and tomorrow, and tomorrow
  I'll have to hear her whining. Bloody hell.
  I thought I said 'Throw physic to the dogs'?
Seyton: I did, my lord. They too have
                  woke refreshed.

        BILL GREENWELL

HIDDEN TREASURES

Verses in which every line contains the concealed name of a poet

With *bunting* threadbare on the hoop-la stall,
Stout *morris*-dancers puffing on the *green*
Outside the *Lamb* and Flag, our festival
Comes to its *swift* conclusion – sombre scene!
The *peacock* spreads his feathers and I yawn.
Our village idiot with his dirty, *gray*
Long-*johns* on (nothing else) crosses the lawn
And disappears. The *young* bloods roar away
In *smart* cars, while the *butler* from the castle,
A *new man* after ten pints, slips his bird
A *pound*, and then assaults her like a parcel.
Boarding her Rolls, the old *squire*'s wife is heard
To say, 'A *ralegh* pleasant afternoon!
I'm *surrey*, though, it had to end *sassoon*.'

PERCY FLARGE

Calleva Atrebatum under February *frost*
Hides *fuller* days of glory of two thousand
                                    years ago.
Graves of Caesar's legions are overgrown and lost
With a *hood* of seedy fodder crops and patches
                                    of wet snow.
To *savage land or* sinecure the
                              mercenaries tramped
Over marshy flats and wheatfields *browning* in
                                    the sun;
The thinnest traces show the roads and *bridges*
                              where they camped:
Over *gray* and mossy wall-remains the raucous
                              children run.

Now the *Austin* and the *Bentley* will bring the
                              legions bold
Where ancient Roman feet would *pound* the way;
In the car-park they will *sit well* wrapped
                              against the cold,
The *hardy* conquering cohorts of today.
At Silchester a *lark in* solitary flight
Makes a *swift* last sortie over military might.

JIM ANTHONY

Her *Bert* has little taste for haute cuisine,
Disparaging her aspic (tongues of *lark in*);
Her wish that he *love peacock*, or tureen
Of *lamb* soup (glacé), won no credit mark in
His 'Best Nosh Guide'. He said, 'Just bring
                                    me *porter*,
A glass, and Bisto *browning* up my gravy.
Your snails would make a Glasgow man
                                    drink water,
Your *hamburger* would turn all straight
                                    hair wavy.
The gourmet in this British *land or* nation
Will never burn his *bridges* when abroad;
A look of *frost* will greet their spiced collation –
A *fry*-up – yes! – all else will be ignored.
In France, my "*Cor!* – *bière* and sarnies" saves
Us from the garlic grasp of foreign *graves*.'

BILL GREENWELL

By Ron, I mean the Greenwood Ron –
                                    you know –
The bloke who pipped *young* Clough for
                                    Revie's job,
Whose *prior* role was playing honest Joe
To Don the *Hood*, who joined the Arab mob.
No touchline *barker* – he's the FA's man,
The theorist, who's learnt to *read* the game –
(While West Ham lose, points out the *hardy* fan,
And Forest come on *strong*!) Have they no shame
These FA cronies, *swift* as dozy snails?
Who will not *crane* their necks to see the mess?
Who *sit well*-placed on boards while soccer fails –
Instead of building *bridges* to success?
But what are *words worth* dealing with
                                    such fools?
Let's *pound* our angry fists and shout:
                                    'Clough rules!'

TIM HOPKINS

CURT CRITICS

A famous three-word criticism of *I am a Camera* **went 'Me no Leica'. Similar criticisms were asked for.**

The Playboy of the Western World: A Paean
in the Erse

M. HYNES

Carrie: on avoiding

KEN WYKE

The Threepenny Opera: Curt, vile

JIM ANTHONY

Under Milk Wood: How the udder half lives

J. TIMSON

Lawrence of Arabia: Just deserts

R. GODDARD

Lady Windermere's Fan: Not I

ROBERT LISTER

Cleopatra: Taylor made by Burton

ERNEST PODS

Othello: Venetian hanky-panky

STANLEY J. SHARPLESS

Roots: Strictly for the suckers

RODDY REDDING

'Tis Pity She's a Whore: Well, since acting's
not her thing . . .
The Boy Friend: Definitely dated
Mary Rose: Me, too – and left

HARRISON EVERARD

Alpha Beta: Gammon
Black Emmanuelle: That's my advice, brothers

DAVID WAGSTAFFE

Citizen Kane: Welles farrago

KEVIN MORRIS

Murder on the Orient Express: Signal failure

TOM DONNELLY

The Three Musketeers: Pathos, Bathos
and D'Artagnan

BARBARA WILCOX

Swan Lake: Tutu awful

DAVID PHILLIPS

'Tis Pity She's a Whore: Gold, frank incest
and murder
St Joan: Rack and Rouen

TOM BREWER

The Royal Hunt of the Sun: Inca hoots
The Changing Room: More pricks than kicks

BRENDON GORSE

8½: Nein!

TIM HOPKINS

Saturday Sunday Monday: Long. Weak end

V. F. CORLEONE

The Sting: Just a B-picture

NICHOLAS HODGSON

THREE IN ONE

**The titles of three well-known books put together so
that they tell a pithy story**

*The Naked Runner; The African Queen; Look
Back in Anger.*

*The Virgin Soldiers; Brief Encounter; Black's
Medical Dictionary.*

TED THOMPSON

*Men Without Women; Portnoy's Complaint; Eyeless
in Gaza.*

G. R. EINDER

The Prime Minister; Decline and Fall; Lord Jim.

*Brave New World; Black Mischief; The Return of
the Native.*

JOHN STANLEY

*The Ragged Trousered Philanthropists; The Nine
Tailors; Lord of the Flies.*

J. A. FRANKLIN

Lord Jim; Girl, 20; Lucky Jim.

GEORGINA HAMMICK

Late Call; A Room of One's Own; Flush.

H. G. TAYLOR

*Whisky Galore; Joy in the Morning; Death in the
Afternoon.*

JOYCE JOHNSON

Windsor Castle; Royal Flash; The Happy Prince.

E. O. PARROTT

*Arabia Deserta; Ivanhoe; How Green Was My
Valley.*

PETER PETERSON

*Gaudy Night; Over the Bridge; And Quiet Flows
the Don.*

MARY HOLTBY

*Five Go Off to Camp; Five Get Into Trouble; The
Secret Seven Mystery.*

GERRY HAMILL

*What's Become of Waring; Down and Out in Paris
and London; Scouting for Boys.*

BOB SCOTT

On the Beach; Jaws; A Farewell to Arms.

BARRY ANTHONY

FROM OUR LOCAL CORRESPONDENT

Auden wrote that 'Poetry makes nothing happen.' News reports proving the contrary were asked for.

The date for the opening of the controversial new town being built in the centre of Bradford has finally been fixed, *writes our Yorkshire correspondent*. The architect, George Higgins, formerly well-known as a long-distance country rambler, has extravagant plans for the ceremony. These are said to include the entry of Mr Higgins in a blazing car, the minting of gold darts for use in the new recreation centre, and the cutting of a ribbon by Mr Higgins with the sword he has been eccentrically wearing throughout the town's construction. At a crowded press conference, Mr Higgins announced that the new town would be called Jerusalem.

WILL BELLENGER

Ron Endaway, shepherd of the hills at Malvern, looked very sheepish as he stood in the dock yesterday, charged with rape.

Miss X, aged 14, denies having made sheep's eyes at him. She told the court Endaway had lured her to some rocks with sweet talk.

'He said he wanted me to live with him and be his love, but he was only after the one thing.'

Ron, she alleged, had tried to pull the wool over her eyes with a flock of promises. These included fragrant posies, a straw belt with amber studs and a table made of solid ivory. He also said he would make her an embroidered kirtle.

But he didn't do any of these things, according to Miss X. Instead, she alleges, Ron proved to be a bit of a ram.

The case continues.

NAOMI MARKS

Hordes of young vandals continued yesterday to descend like locusts on Britain's parks and gardens, stripping rosebushes of their buds. Hampton Court's head gardener, Mr Fred Potts (53), who lost thousands of buds in yesterday's raids, could offer no explanation. 'They looked an educated class of person, not your usual yobbo,' he said. 'Some were even waving books.' Private rosegrower Mr Sid Mould (53) of Harrow, whose blooms regularly win awards, told reporters: 'I'm sick as a parrot. The blighters stripped my Ena Harkness. The wife says we should get an alsatian.' A spokesman for the Red Cross (53) appealed urgently for blood donors to meet increased demand for transfusions following multiple thorn injuries. Meanwhile, sociologists at Essex University are seeking Home Office funds for a research project entitled 'Rosebud gathering – an existential response to gerontophobic alienation?'

R. D. CONDON

Colour it cherry-red and call it Death-Wish Valley – that's the message as Spring comes to the sleepy county of Shropshire.

Cherry trees blossom as murder and suicide rates spiral and hundreds of young men join the Forces daily.

Shreswbury's recruiting officer said yesterday: 'Many applicants say they will sign on only if they can be posted to Crossmaglen.'

They blame the local girls. 'The birds bugger us about,' one disgruntled Shropshire lad told me in Ludlow's swinging Land of Lost Content disco last night. 'Playing blokes off against each other and that. There's knife fights here every night.'

With so many young Salopians murder or suicide victims, serving life sentences or away in the Forces, the birth rate has fallen dramatically.

Shropshire may soon be known as the Deserted County.

IAN SAINSBURY

Locals are puzzled by a sudden influx of self-sufficiency-seekers to a lake island in the Irish outback.

More puzzling still, the good-lifers seem to have a strangely identical set of priorities, though they deny any previous knowledge of one another's intentions or any copy-catting.

Each newcomer – they come singly – has built himself a small clay and wattle cabin, planted nine rows of beans and installed a beehive; each is obsessed with sound, colour, peace like some latter-day hippie; each even claims to have heard the lapping of these waters, these droning bees, singing crickets, winging linnets in far-away city streets. They go on about lit-up nights and purpled noons, too.

Can they have been attracted to Innisfree by some particularly intoxicating brand of 'Morning Dew'? If so, no-one's telling!

MAY DAY

LIMITED VOCABULARIES

**Extracts of verse using only four-letter words,
and those of a seemly nature**

Shun love, wise maid, lest love turn into hate;
When joys leap high, what long dark fall
        must wait!
Gaze over some fair pool, your eyes will miss
That weed deep down – mean love acts just
        like this.
Soft lure, base wile, sour trap – list arts
        more grim,
Each fits this vile name, love; they sink
        that swim.
When Eros' evil dart aims true, folk reel;
Once made, that open sore what balm will heal?
Play ball with love, alas, love wins that game;
Pipe, love will call your tune, your wild
        note tame.
Free, love will bind your feet; pray, then,
        poor fool,
Whom fire, when felt, must burn – take heed,
        keep cool.
Mark well this gate: pass here, love asks
        full toll . . .
You'd risk your body? Love will have
        your soul.

    MOYRA BLYTH

Busy with cars, this huge high road
 Goes slow, then fast with many hops:
Long keep them safe from harm, kind cops,
 Help over here each tiny toad.
Ugly they seem – ugly like work
 Some poet says (damn-fool idea!)
That Avon bard knew that they peer
 From eyes like gems ('Fair uses lurk
When life gets sour') What more? we've read
 That foul bent hags lick soup . . . vile fare!
Such food will make cats sick, that ne'er
 Felt pang when poor dumb fish were dead.
Then come, join paws, loud laud that code
That lets them pass – thus long live toad!

    MARTIN FAGG

Come into yard, Maud,
Wait near gate,
Come into yard, Maud,
Meet your fate.
Lips like wine,
Baby mine.

Grey dawn soon,
Bats have fled,
Exit moon,
Salt tear shed.
Come, fair maid –
Ever been laid?

STANLEY J. SHARPLESS

DON'T SIGN HERE

To counter the book-signing fad, competitors were asked to provide blurbs describing authors whom no one could possibly want to meet.

Norman T. B. Dunster – 'old TB' – is surely unique among writers today. From his craggy, tortured features, so savagely maimed by the acne that was the motivation of his first novel *Hide My Face* (1937), right down to his surgical boots, he is a man who stands out from others at a glance. The characteristic stubborness – so often mistaken for aggression – with which he refuses to this day to acknowledge increasing deafness was already much in evidence in *Holding Firm*, his second and some say his most noteworthy work, finally published in 1971. Dunster's other writings include *Who Am I?* (1975), a tetralogy about his desperate search for himself, and a series of essays on Mormonism, Scientology and the Moon movement.

DAVID SIMPSON

Gaspard Leprechaun was the pseudonym chosen by Jeff Stringer to celebrate his consumption of 75 cigarettes a day and his contraction of a highly infectious form of leprosy in the Angolan brothel that formed the setting of his first novel, *Itch*. Ever anxious to convey an authentic setting by experiencing it in its entirety, he then spent three years in a Peruvian TB sanatorium researching for *Cough*, the second volume of his tragicomic trilogy. *Snore* is the third and perhaps the most devastating: after indulging in every form of animal husbandry known to the Ikbolo tribe, Leprechaun finally succeeded in contracting tryponosomiasis and, during the brief lucid intervals granted by the sleeping sickness, he set down a harrowing narrative full of compassion and serenity – a truly germinal work.

V. F. CORLEONE

A Bishop's by-blow and now an Archdeacon's helpmeet, Hermione Crypt has enjoyed unlimited opportunity for perfecting the wickedly observant characterisation ('She impales her creatures quite pitilessly upon the page' – *Church Times*) that informs her series of superbly grisly clerical whodunits (*Blessed Sod*, *The Soak of Peterborough*, *A Clyster in the Cloister*, *Sick Dean*, *Chapter and Worse*, *Loaded Canon* and now this, her latest, *Psalter and Battery*). But her experience has not been confined to the poisoned chalices of the Cathedral Close. Far from it. Apart from sitting on the Royal Commission on Inner City Decay, she has plied a trenchant pen on such consuming topics as *Bestiality: A Christian View*; while her *Incest in South Worcestershire: Seven Years Field-Work Surveyed* (Pershore Polytechnic Press) is already by way of being a socio-sexual classic . . .

PAUL PITCHCROFT

INDEX